CW00972399

Roots of Transformation

Roots of Transformation

Negotiating the Dynamics of Growth

Robin Stockitt

FOREWORD BY
Bishop Ken Good

 CASCADE *Books* · Eugene, Oregon

ROOTS OF TRANSFORMATION
Negotiating the Dynamics of Growth

Copyright © 2015 Robin Stockitt. All rights reserved. Except for brief quotations in critical publications or reviews, no part of this book may be reproduced in any manner without prior written permission from the publisher. Write: Permissions. Wipf and Stock Publishers, 199 W. 8th Ave., Suite 3, Eugene, OR 97401.

Cascade Books
An Imprint of Wipf and Stock Publishers
199 W. 8th Ave., Suite 3
Eugene, OR 97401

www.wipfandstock.com

ISBN 13: 978-1-4982-2078-1

Cataloguing-in-Publication Data

Stockitt, Robin

    Roots of transformation : negotiating the dynamics of growth / Robin Stockitt

    xii + 122 p. ; 23 cm. Includes bibliographical references.

    ISBN 13: 978-1-4982-2078-1

    1. Spiritual formation. 2. Spiritual life—Christianity. I. Title.

BV4509.5 S70 2015

Manufactured in the U.S.A.   10/16/2015

With thanks to Stephen Broadbent for permission to use the photograph of his sculpture "Water of Life."

For Joni

Contents

Illustrations

Foreword

ROBIN STOCKITT IS A hands-on pastor and priest. His ministerial gifts are effective in a parish setting, and people on the street as well as in the pew are responsive to his pastoral care, to his communication skills, and to his leadership. It is all the more interesting, therefore, to see how a parish practitioner applies intellectual rigor and broad reading to their experience of practical and pastoral issues of life and faith.

In the pages that follow, Robin grapples with a fundamental question that must surely be of relevance to all involved in Christian leadership: *Why is it that some people's experience of faith in Christ leads to a deep and enduring life-transformation whereas for others the change seems much less apparent?* In his exploration of the hidden dynamics of transformation, Robin has identified some key factors that can either be a hindrance or a help to a Christian's spiritual transformation, depending on the extent to which those factors are acknowledged and dealt with.

In the Diocese of Derry and Raphoe the focus of our mission is: *Transforming Community, Radiating Christ.* So Robin's examination of the place that culture, tradition, language, and discomfort can play in facilitating or limiting personal transformation is one that I warmly welcome. He raises important questions about the part that key relationships can play—particularly with one's parents, but also with significant others—in giving or withholding permission and encouragement for us to change.

It is made clear at the outset that this work has emerged more from pastoral observations and conversations than from qualitative research; nor does it intend to provide techniques of how-to-do-transformation. This is an exploration of seven important themes, any of which could profitably be further explored in a process of engagement towards personal growth and spiritual transformation. In each section there is a blend of biblical reflection, applied insights from significant authors, and life experiences of contemporary interviewees.

I have found the material insightful, practical, enriching, and relevant—both to my life and to my ministry, and I have every reason to believe that you will do so, too.

—Ken Good

Bishop of Derry and Raphoe
(Church of Ireland)

Acknowledgments

I AM DEEPLY GRATEFUL to the individuals who willingly agreed to be interviewed for this project. They allowed me to hear their stories and were willing to make themselves vulnerable. I am also thankful to Bishop Ken Good (Diocese of Derry and Raphoe, Church of Ireland) for his encouragement and for his willingness to write the foreword to this book.

Introduction

THE CHRISTIAN GOSPEL MAKES daring, bold claims. These claims are so outrageous as to appear foolish, even naive, to the uninitiated. The foundational claim is that Christ came to announce the appearance of the kingdom of God here on earth and that this kingdom has an utterly transforming quality about it. It is so powerful that only an array of metaphorical images can do justice to the range and texture of its reach. This kingdom, contained in a narrative in which Jesus Christ is the central character, is like yeast that silently spreads unnoticed through society. It is so precious that it is akin to a lost coin owned by a poor widow that must be retrieved with the utmost urgency. Or it is like light that cannot—must not—be hidden. "You are that light," Jesus says to the ragged collection of listeners one day; "you are also the salt of the earth, and you are a city set on a hill."

Such metaphorical descriptions of Christian identity were offered as an invitation to view oneself afresh. Those first disciples of Christ were to perceive their true selves as loftier and more significant than they had ever thought possible. "It is through you," says Jesus, to the motley crowd in front of him on a hill one afternoon, "that the transformation of the world will happen." Likewise, when Jesus taught people how to pray, the template that he offered contained the apparently innocuous phrase "may your kingdom come and your will be done on earth as it is in heaven." This prayer raises the expectation that something of the quality and beauty of heaven (however we may conceive what this is) may appear, or may arise on earth. What an extraordinary supplication! How would we ever know if this has happened? What are the hallmarks, the tell-tale signs that a foretaste of heaven has made an appearance on earth?

The apostle Paul was not averse to making sweeping statements too about the power of his message, as can be heard in this phrase from his second letter to the Corinthians.

> And we all, who with unveiled faces contemplate the Lord's glory, are being transformed into his image with ever-increasing glory, which comes from the Lord, who is the Spirit.[1]

In this one sentence Paul claims that as the Corinthian church contemplates the glory of God, the same glory will awaken a process of transformation in the lives of ordinary folk that can only be described as glorious. Few of us would dare lay claim to such a depiction of our lives as we consider our own stuttering, faltering, journey of Christian discipleship. Yet this is precisely what Paul is claiming, and it is this bewildering process of transformation that simultaneously beckons and challenges us. The power to transform is at the heart of the Christian story, which centres around the story of the person of Jesus Christ. The claim is that Jesus, the divine Son of God, has entered into the hell of human existence, he has plumbed its depths and he has absorbed within himself the pain, the tragedy, and the sheer evil that lurks within each of us. It is because of this already accomplished task that we—frail, pathetic, and caged humanity—can step out into the glorious freedom of the children of God. That is the claim, and it is a daring one indeed.

It is not hard to find examples in history that such transformational claims are valid. One could cite the story of William Wilberforce whose deeply held Christian convictions impelled him to campaign for the abolition of slavery for many years. His efforts were rewarded in 1833 with the passing of the Slavery Abolition Act, just three days before his death. Additionally the story of

---

1. 2 Cor 3:18.

Dietrich Bonhoeffer is replete with examples of the transformative power of faith in the most demanding of circumstances. Bonhoeffer, a German pastor in the 1930s, chose to actively oppose Hitler's regime as an expression of his deep Christian convictions. His decision to resist the power of the Third Reich resulted in his arrest in 1943, his imprisonment, and his subsequent execution in Flossenbürg concentration camp on 9th April 1945. During his incarceration he wrote a number of letters depicting his life, his emotional state, and his theological reflections. In one of his letters, composed on 11 April 1944, he writes:

> I heard someone say yesterday that the last years had been completely wasted as far as he was concerned. I am very glad that I have never had that feeling, even for a moment. Nor have I ever regretted my decision[2] in the summer of 1939, for I am firmly convinced—however strange it may seem—that my life has followed a straight and unbroken course, at any rate in its outward conduct. It has been an uninterrupted enrichment of experience, for which I can only be thankful.[3]

Yet Christian history is not always so inspiring and life-giving. There are many instances of a huge disconnect between the extravagant claims of the Christian message and its out-working in reality. The disconnect arises when the transformation that should—indeed must—accompany the good news, does not appear to arise, or at least is so imperceptible that society remains locked in adversarial and competitive existence. The story of Rwanda is a case in point. In 1994 the tiny land-locked country of Rwanda was known to be a profoundly Christian nation with 85 percent of the population in regular church attendance on Sundays. Yet due to a complex web of political and tribal maneuverings the country imploded and in the space of 100 days approximately 800,000 people were slaughtered in a vicious civil war, often at the hands of ordinary civilians armed with machetes.

---

2. Referring to the decision to return to Germany after having lived in America.

3. Bonhoeffer, *Letters and Papers from Prison*, 88.

Stories emerged of neighbors who had lived peacefully side-by-side in the same village for years suddenly turning upon each other in deadly violence.

The extraordinary aspect of this tragedy is that it was Christians and church leaders who were part of the corporate culpability. One of the Rwandan bishops involved in the national catastrophe, Bishop Phocas Nikwigize, has written about the genocide in retrospect.

> What happened in 1994 was something very human. When someone attacks you, you must defend yourself. Within such as situation you forget you are a Christian; you are then first of all a human being. As in any war, there are spies. In order for the rebels to be successful in their coup d'état, they had accomplices everywhere. These were collaborators, friends of the enemy. They were in contact with the rebels. They had to be eliminated so that they could not betray any more.[4]

This profoundly honest admission suggests that the transformative power of the gospel in this Christian nation was simply not strong enough, nor deep enough, to overcome tribal bonds. During those 100 days there was something profoundly impotent about the way in the which the Christian community faced that immense challenge. It is not my intention, however, to point an accusing finger at those who were complicit, but rather to assert that the spiritual dynamics that allowed this tragedy to unfold are contained in each of us.

EXPLORING TRANSFORMATION

Towards the latter part of his letter to the Romans, Paul writes about the necessity—the obligation even—of transformation. For much of this letter Paul has argued that the Christian message has the power to reconcile differing tribes, ethnicities, and cultures into one gloriously diverse new community. The former suspicions

4. Semujanga, *Religious Discourse and the Making of Identity*, 77.

and prejudices can now be laid aside and the emerging fledgling church, surrounded by a hostile, imperious culture, can learn to view itself as a subversively different, radically new community of very ordinary people. This is why, after eleven chapters of dense theological persuasion, he writes: *"Be transformed through the renewal of your mind."*[5] What an enigmatic phrase this is. Be transformed; passive voice. It has the sound of consent to it. It suggests surrendering to a process that takes place continually, secretly, covertly even. It hints at the possibility that this transformation is being offered to us and our response is to welcome it, to permit that process to be applied to us. Yet the simple word "be" at the beginning of the phrase is an imperative, an instruction. There is the hint of urgency about this, for it implies that transformation is no leisure option, a take-it-or-leave-it choice. "Be transformed" has the cadence of a clarion call, a summons to consciously, intentionally, deliberately move away from a place of stagnation towards a place of dynamic, deep renewal.

But the second half of the phrase brings in a strong active component—through the renewal of your mind. Could this mean simply the strenuous task of engaging in the power of positive thinking? A purely rational, intellectual process that requires the determination to examine one's mind in the cool light of day leading—hey presto!—to renewal? Yet we all know that the mind is not so easily tamed; it flits around like a butterfly from flower to flower, impossible to control and with a life, seemingly, of its own.

For the apostle Paul who wrote these words, I suspect that he was saying something far more profound than simply "think new thoughts." Paul, the educated Hebrew, steeped in the Jewish Scriptures from birth, would have known that the mind and the heart were not two separate distinct entities. In the Hebrew language the word for heart (*lēb*) means the totality of one's being. It includes our emotional life, our thinking, and the murmurings of our souls. *Lēb* was the place of great wisdom and, intriguingly, also the place where we can so easily deceive ourselves.

5. Rom 12:2.

So what did Paul mean by transformation? Was he merely urging higher moral development, a more pure form of holiness, an escape from the trials and travails of this life? I suspect this was very far from his thinking. He had already lived that kind of austere life prior to that defining moment on the Damascus road when everything had changed forever. He had lived a cold, rigid, defensive form of holiness. It carried within it the seeds of jealousy and violence and it depended fundamentally on a fastidious adherence to law. It was not a lifestyle that was life-giving.

This is why transformation is not to be understood as "trying to be a better person." It is not about a form of moral rectitude that is life-sapping, colorless, and bland. The Greek word that is translated here is *metamorphoō* and it is a word that is rarely used in the New Testament. It is translated as "transfiguration" on the occasion when Christ climbed to the top of a mountain accompanied by three disciples and experienced the *shekina* of God descending upon him such that his whole face and demeanor was utterly different. There was a kind of holy presence, an aura of the transcendent, such that those who witnessed the event were rendered virtually speechless. It is this same word, *metamorphoō*, that Paul uses in his second letter to the Corinthians where he depicts the result of our faces turned towards the face of God. When our faces encounter the face of God, it is a holy moment of metamorphosis, glorious, sublime, filled with awe.

This is why transformation must be understood to be intrinsically beautiful. It is the kind of word that we use to describe the way in which a caterpillar becomes—through the stage of pupae—an astonishing, delicate, and beautifully formed butterfly. Transformation is the only way to describe the way in which a lump of coal becomes—through heat and pressure—a diamond or the way in which a piece of grit inside an oyster turns into a pearl. It is the emergence of beauty from ugliness; it is the creation of something sublime. Fyodor Dostoevsky wrote in *The Idiot*, that "only beauty will save the world." Beauty has a redemptive quality about it. In a similar vein, the philosopher John Macmurray writes in *Freedom in the Modern World*,

I am inclined to think that the worst feature of modern life is its failure to believe in beauty. . . . If we want to make the world better, the main thing we have to do is make it more beautiful.[6]

I believe that this kind of beautiful transformation is another way of expressing what Jesus once said: "I have come that you might have life and have it to the full." It is precisely this abundant fullness that transformation ushers us towards. Life in all its abundance has a scarcely definable quality about it, but maybe this list captures some of its essence.

Free, grateful, attentive, gentle, forgiving, spontaneous, joyful, available, vulnerable, healed, creative, fearless, firm, rooted, open, secure, loved, giving, receiving, holding, waiting, listening, patient, understanding, trusting, connected, included, reconciled, content, beautiful.

Perhaps this is also a way of depicting the character of Christ himself. By way of contrast, a life that does not consent to such transformation runs the risk of missing out on abundance. How could one paint a picture of such a life? Maybe this list describes some of its qualities:

Wary, defensive, caged, cramped, fearful, guilty, shamed, driven, unworthy, harsh, jagged, prickly, blaming, hiding, judgmental, busy, resisting, resentful, demanding, distant, guarded, suspicious, limited, victim, insecure, separate, disconnected, alone, accusing, discontent, ugly.

The puzzle that this book attempts to address is to offer some ways of understanding why on some occasions the transformation of an individual or the transformation of society due to the influence of the Christian message appears to be deep, enduring, and inspiring; whilst on other occasions there seems to be no transformation whatsoever. How is it that some people in a church community can be profoundly changed by an experience of God and others in that same community remain untouched and unmoved? What are the dynamics that govern this?

6. Macmurray, *Freedom in the Modern World*, 45.

It may be argued at this point that the answer is quite simple and one simply needs to revert to biblical categories of speech. Repentance, for example, is the beginning of all transformation, and the ongoing, sanctifying work of the Holy Spirit ensures that the process of transformation never stops. This combined with a eucharistic lifestyle of thanksgiving leads inexorably towards transformed individuals. These answers contain statements that are of course true, yet it is also entirely valid to insist that we need to be pretty specific about what we are repenting of. What is it that we are turning away from when we repent? And whilst it is right to insist on the Holy Spirit's activity, it is also correct to say that the Spirit is at work in and through our human structures and within our own psychological make-up.

The opportunities for growth are perennially present. They can consist in those significant moments of decision making that have huge consequences. Such moments happen rarely in one's life and they occur not simply when the choice of career or marriage partner presents itself. They can occur at times when great courage or self sacrifice are demanded. Most of us have been inspired by those who have faced life threatening illnesses or tragic losses with dignity and grace. Yet opportunities for growth usually come in smaller packages, in those seemingly insignificant actions and events that can so easily go unnoticed. Experience on its own does not transform us; it merely affords us with the raw material from which transformation can be hewn. On each new occasion and each fresh experience we are required to construct for ourselves an interpretation, to derive meaning and significance, if indeed such can be found. We are always faced with the choice to take a risky step of faith forward or to retreat into the safety of the known and the comfortable. Growth therefore always involves an assessment of risk. What is the risk of losing something precious to me if I choose to take this opportunity to grow? And simultaneously, what is the possible future gain if a step of faith is taken? This is the process of weighing up the balance of loss and gain and then—only after this assessment has been made—making a choice. Both braking and accelerating mechanisms are involved. These mechanisms are explored in the seven chapters in this book.

As part of research for this project, I have conducted a number of lengthy interviews, with the intention of hearing how each person has experienced some sense of transformation and how they have been able to reflect upon that process. I have selected these people because the signs of genuine transformation in each of them is evident. Each person was asked to address five initial questions. These are:

- Looking back over the past ten years or so can you notice any signs of transformation in your life?

- If so, has there been a particular trigger or set of triggers that have been the cause?

- Over this period have you noticed how your emotional life has changed?

- Over this period have you noticed how your thinking has changed?

- Over this period has your perception of God changed?

This has not been a carefully controlled piece of qualitative research, but rather a set of questions that have formed the basis of a conversation. The more relaxed and informal the conversation, the more revealing and vulnerable have been the responses. The questions were designed to be merely the starting point for discussion, with the tacit understanding that supplementary questions could—and always were—put forward. The apparently simple set of questions proved to be very challenging for each participant for they demanded the capacity for honest self reflection. They attempted to address the cognitive, the emotional, and the spiritual components of the transformation process and the answers offered were, without exception, contained within narrative accounts of experiences. From time to time I will refer to these participants by their pseudonyms—Mary, Michael, Lucy, Sarah, David, John, and Alison.

What emerged from these conversations were a number of recurrent themes. It is these themes that form the substance of this book and I offer them as the roots of transformation. I intend to explore each one not by proposing any how-to-do-transformation techniques but by suggesting that transformation requires the demanding process of engagement with the questions that they raise. How these issues are explored, negotiated, resolved, or avoided has significant implications for enabling or hindering the process of growth. I have clustered these issues around seven areas and for each area of exploration I have chosen one dialogue partner whose writings may prove to be both informative and illustrative.

Permission

This opening chapter addresses the question of whether or not we possess the internal permission to develop, to grow, and to submit to the process of transformation that the Holy Spirit constantly seeks to elicit. When Jesus issued his call to those first disciples on the shores of the lake, "come follow me," it was a challenge to form a new attachment. That same call can still be heard today and it instantly finds an echo in our previous experiences of forming attachments. To choose to heed the call of Christ requires, therefore, the internal permission to form a deep and enduring attachment to him, which might in turn necessitate a realignment of all the other attachments in our lives. Permission to change is rooted in our early experiences of attachment to our parents and it is because of this that we will dialogue with the work of the Clinical Psychologist John Bowlby, whose work on Attachment and Loss has proven to be of immense value in understanding human development.

Discomfort

This chapter deals with the role that discomfort plays in our lives. Pain stops us in our tracks. Like a stone in our shoe we simply have to stop and examine what is so uncomfortable. This God-given braking mechanism comes in the form of opportunity to form a relationship with pain, and the outcome of this relationship will determine whether occasions of discomfort have the potential to form the stepping stone for growth or not. Times of discomfort, as C. S. Lewis discovered, can be transformational occasions, as we will explore in conversation with him.

Narrative

Stories form the warp and woof of our lives. This chapter examines the way in which we tell ourselves and others stories about who we are. All of our lives are constructed around the narratives about ourselves that we sincerely believe to be true. These narratives are woven into our memories and define who we are and who we would like to be. Our narratives have the capacity both to open up and to close down the possibilities for transformation. The transformative declaration of Christ—"the kingdom of God is already among you"[7]—can be heard as the chance to step inside an alternative narrative, to inhabit, as it were, a different story. The French philosopher Paul Ricoeur spent much of his life exploring how narrative and human identity are interwoven. He will be our guide in this chapter.

Language

In the beginning, God spoke, and the world came into existence. The Word became flesh and dwelt amongst. The significance of language as transformative utterance cannot therefore be overstated. It is through the means of language that alternative paradigms of existence can be imagined. The story of Jesus is couched in linguistic structures that invite, attract, and entice us to be transformed. The work of Ludwig Wittgenstein explores how language usage is a game that has its own grammar and that grammar is rooted in the earthy, real experiences of human existence. The insights of

7. Luke 17:21.

Wittgenstein may help us understand more fully how the prophetic, imaginative language of Scripture can act magnetically upon us.

Culture

Culture may seem to be a strange inclusion in this array of issues to face. Surely Christian transformation is about the transcendence of cultural limitation; it is about the breaking in of this beautiful alternative space that Jesus referred to as "The kingdom of heaven"—right? The reality of our lives, however, is that each of us is rooted in our own specific culture from which we have emerged and which continues to shape who we are today. The transformative power of the gospel is simultaneously incarnated deeply within the diversity of human cultures and also profoundly subversive of each them. This paradoxical relationship between the call to live as responsible citizens in society and the parallel demand to challenge the very foundational assumptions of civic life is a tricky one to negotiate. The relationship between Christ and culture has been extensively explored by H. Richard Niebuhr and it is with some of his writings that we will dialogue.

Other

"No man is an island" wrote John Donne famously in 1624. The otherness of our existence is part of our created DNA for it is not good for any of us to live alone. For many of us transformation is quite simply impossible without the support, encouragement, and challenge of a significant other. When such a person appears on the horizon of our lives it is truly a divine gift, for they possess the power to call us forth to become more than we ever imagined possible. At other times, it is through the community of others that we find ourselves being magnetically drawn towards a freer more creative space. When Jesus named his church as his *ekklēsia*, he was describing those who had been "called out"[8] to become

---

8 *Ekklēsia* is *ek* "out from"; *kaleō*, "to call."

a community of healing, reconciliation, and transformation. A significant other may even be someone who has profoundly and deeply hurt us, such that we are determined to be utterly different from *that kind* of other that has faced us. And perhaps most profoundly, it is through standing before the face of The Wholly Other that moments of transformation can occur. The Jewish theologian Martin Buber will be our conversation partner in this chapter, drawing on the insights of his most memorable work, *I and Thou*.

Silence

The final chapter will explore the role of silence in the journey of transformation. The earliest exponents of stillness and the contemplative life—the desert fathers and mothers of the third and fourth centuries—knew well the vagaries and complexities of the human heart in the search for God. It was *only* through silence, they argued, that the transformation of the soul can take place. For each of us silence is an ever-present space into which we may choose to tread. As those early desert contemplatives discovered, it can also be a scary place filled with our own demons amid the swirling chaos of thoughts and feelings. We will draw upon the accumulated wisdom of these early pioneers who explored the silent land of contemplative prayer.

Before exploring each of these more fully, it may be helpful to place one biblical story on the table as a paradigm for all that follows. It is the story that is usually only recited once a year, during the season of Christmas, and then, sadly, it recedes from our collective awareness. It is the account of the angel Gabriel's visit to Mary to announce these astonishing words, "you will be with child and give birth to a son and you are to give him the name Jesus." The gift of life, the very life of God, is implanted in Mary. It is not offered to her, it is non-contractual; it is unconditional; it is simply given. The story unfolds by recording the range of her responses, from fear to incredulity to acceptance. Her response to that which is already given permits the process of gestation to take place. The way in which Luke has positioned this story at the beginning of his gospel implies that it is paradigmatic for the way in which God engages with humanity; that the divine initiative is characterized by utter givenness, a givenness that is entirely independent of the human response that follows. When Luke says that Mary is highly favored, he uses the Greek word *charitoō*, which has this flavor of meaning:

> to make graceful, charming, lovely, agreeable: to pursue with grace, to compass with favor, to honor.[9]

Mary was honored by this gift, raised up from her lowly status to a place where she could embrace the divine gift with joyful delight. The only other place where this verb is used is in Ephesians 1:5–6, where Paul writes

> he predestined us for adoption to sonship through Jesus Christ, in accordance with his pleasure and will—to the praise of his glorious grace, which he has freely given (*charitoō*) us in the One he loves.

It is as if the honoring of Mary at the moment of encounter with Gabriel is a pattern for the way in which each of us is honored and graced in Christ. Our response to the gift of being included into the life of God is therefore one of gestation. How we each engage in that gestation process is what this book is all about. It is a journey that demands the totality of our being, requiring a re-examination of our reflex patterns of rational thought, an honest assessment of our emotional life, and a revisiting of our volitional choices. All of these are brought together to transform our store of knowledge about ourselves and the God with whom we are inextricably connected.

These seven themes are not intended to be the final word on transformation. It is my conviction that these themes cannot be negotiated sequentially, nor can we ever say that we have ever fully completed the work that each one demands. Human experiences do not arrive in nice neat packages labelled "narrative" or "language." Life is far messier than that and it is a demanding exercise

9. Accordance Biblical Concordance (Thayer).

to unpick the tangled skeins that lie within each of us in order to make sense of the transforming process. Many of us may hesitate to declare that any transformation has taken place over the years, and even if some signs of growth are discernible it is a brave soul who is able to understand precisely how that change has come about. Thank God that we are not left to make sense of this all on our own. The work of the indwelling Holy Spirit of God, the midwife of change, is akin to that of an artist who inhabits each of these themes in all their uncomfortable, disordered jumble and seeks to weave a beautiful tapestry out of them all.

1

Permission

I HAVE LONG BEEN fascinated by the seemingly innocuous, touching story[1] of the twelve-year-old boy Jesus finding himself stranded in a huge bustling city while his frantic parents scour the band of pilgrims searching for the whereabouts of their son. What an odd story to be selected by Luke to be included in his gospel! It is the only tiny snippet of information about the childhood and approaching adolescence of Jesus that the Gospels offer us. It is a very human story, ordinary and earthy in its honesty. It is a story that some parents could perhaps also recount when their own child suddenly became lost in a busy supermarket or shopping centre. However, in this biblical account there is an oddness about it. It seems to be rather unimportant, a piece of trivia from a life that is usually narrated in terms of miracles, extraordinary storytelling, suffering, and rising to new life. What did Luke think he was doing in offering this morsel, this tidbit of information sandwiched as it is between the presentation of Christ in the temple at the age of eight days and his adult appearance at the time of John the Baptist?

One could rather easily interpret the story as an example of typical childish irresponsibility. Here is a young boy who is seized by a spontaneous impulse to dart into the temple and engage in some intellectual jousting with the academy. He is too immature to realize the distress he might cause to Joseph and Mary, unable as yet to make the link between actions taken now and reaping the

1. Luke 2:41–52.

consequences later. Anyone who has had any dealings with young boys around the time of puberty will know how ungainly and awkward they can be.

Yet I believe that something far more important and profound is happening here; something that everyone at some time in their lives has to face for themselves. It is the question of attachment. Until this point in the earthly life of Christ he had, one must presume, an ordinary childhood within the care and discipline of Joseph and Mary. This would have demanded adherence to the family codes of practice and an honoring of his parents' intrinsic dignity. Yet now there is an apparent rupture, the entry of anxiety, panic, and irritation at the young boy Jesus. It is clear that Jesus had made a choice that would send a clear signal about the direction that he would take in his life. The choice was quite simply whether he was to remain within the orbit of Joseph and Mary or to step away and enter the temple. He chose the latter, without—it would seem—consultation or permission. It has resonances with his apparently alarming injunction uttered years later, that unless his followers "hate their mother and father," they cannot be his disciple. And there are surely similarities with the story of the man who wanted to follow Christ, but first wanted to go and bury his father. "Let the dead bury the dead," was the cold reply from Jesus.

How can we interpret the decision of the boy Jesus when faced with the choice to return home with Mary and Joseph or remain in the city with the religious leaders? One must assume that this cameo is an intentional inclusion by Luke in the construction of his gospel narrative. It is no accident therefore that it is included in Scripture for it is a pivotal moment both in the life of Christ himself and in the narrative flow Luke's composition.

One way of interpreting the incident is with reference to a psychological model known as Attachment Theory, first proposed over sixty years ago by the British psychologist John Bowlby. But why Bowlby? one might ask. Why choose him from amongst the huge range of developmental psychologists that are available? The answer lies in the way in which Jesus frames the call of discipleship. "Come follow me!" he declares boldly, "but remember" (one might add by way of further explanation) "that if you heed this call it will demand a radical rethink of all your current attachments. It might mean renouncing that which is most dear to you, it will demand a reorientation towards me and thus a repositioning of other relationships." The call of Christ is essentially a call to make a deep, daring, and enduring connection with him. It is this profoundly subversive attachment that automatically raises questions about the relative importance of all other relationships. The call to follow Christ and remain intimately attached to him creates immediate echoes within us of forming familial attachments. A resonance can be detected within that speaks of ancient memories of early attachments and all the emotional baggage that comes with that memory. Heeding the call of Christ is no simple matter. It challenges and reframes all previous human attachments and places them under a new spotlight. The one man who has done most in exploring the way on which our attachments are formed, emerge, and metamorphose over time is John Bowlby.

In 1950 Bowlby was invited by the World Health Organization to advise on the mental health of homeless children. He spent years researching the effects of separation in young children in the aftermath of the Second World War and his findings led him to conclude that the nature of the attachment between mother and child was pivotal in shaping the subsequent psychological health of children. His initial findings led him to the conclusion that

> What is believed to be essential for mental health is that the infant and young child should experience a warm, intimate and continuous relationship with his mother (or permanent mother substitute) in which both find satisfaction and enjoyment. . . . [I]t is believed that observation of how a very young child behaves towards his mother, both in her presence and especially in her absence, can greatly contribute to our understanding of personality development.[2]

What was so revolutionary about Bowlby's work is that he started his research from an entirely new standpoint. Up until this

2. Bowlby, *Attachment Vol. 1*, 12.

point, the influence of Freud upon psychoanalytical research had been immense and the accepted approach to understanding human psychology had been to start with the presenting pathology and then work backwards towards early childhood experiences. Bowlby did not do this. He began with observing how infants and young children behave and interact with their mothers in healthy situations and in situations where there was a severance or disruption of the maternal child relationship. From these early observations he was able to predict how psychological disturbances might unfold in future adult life. Over the years his ground-breaking insights have been developed and honed by clinical psychologists[3] such that Attachment Theory now identifies four main clusters of attachment types. These are:

- secure attachment
- anxious-preoccupied attachment
- dismissive-avoidant attachment
- fearful-avoidant attachment

The healthiest form of attachment is one that is secure. This means that both parent and child are able to give and receive love unconditionally. There exists a deep knowing from both sides that the relationship is robust, enduring, intimate, affirming, and respectful. From such a secure base individuals can develop and mature without undue anxiety about the relationship. It means that risks can be taken, challenges accepted, failures experienced, and successes enjoyed, secure in the knowledge that the attachment relationship is capable of being maintained. There is an unconditionality about this kind of attachment. Success, failure, prestige, adulation, and disappointment make no difference to the quality of the relationship. There are no preconditions and not the slightest whiff of anything contractual. A secure attachment might mean that an individual grows up adopting exactly the same values, beliefs, and lifestyle of their parents. Conversely they might travel an

3. For example, Ainsworth and Bowlby, *Child Care and the Growth of Love*; Ainsworth, Blehar, Waters, and Wall, *Patterns of Attachment*.

entirely different path through life. Whatever direction is chosen, the attachment remains safe.

I surmise that it was precisely this kind of secure attachment that Jesus enjoyed with Joseph and Mary. Luke writes that Jesus *submitted himself* to them upon his return to Nazareth,[4] an indication that his extended stay in Jerusalem was no act of adolescent rebellion. So what was going on then when Jesus quietly deviated from the throng of returning pilgrims and entered the temple courts alone? I suggested that this was a pivotal moment of attachment conflict. To whom did he have a deeper allegiance—to his earthly parents or to his heavenly Father? His decision to enter his Father's house (the temple) was not a rejection of parental attachment but a new ordering of priority. Although Jesus was the incarnate Son and thus perfectly holy, he was also fully human and as such needed to go through the normal, ordinary process of maturation. This is precisely what Luke states when he writes that Jesus *grew in wisdom*. Wisdom, by its very nature, is acquired through reflection upon the experiences of life. It does not come down from heaven to us in one single installment. The choice of Jesus to enter the temple courts instead of returning home with the others was crucial for his own personal development. It signaled to Joseph and Mary that he was prepared to be radically obedient to the call of his heavenly Father and that this vocation might bring him into tension with his human relationships. It is no surprise then to find that once the ministry of Jesus begins some twenty years later, he repeatedly returns to the need to consider how family ties impinge upon discipleship choices. Consider for example this startling saying of Jesus in the Gospel of Luke:

> If anyone comes to me and does not hate his own father and mother and wife and children and brothers and sisters, yes, and even his own life, he cannot be my disciple.[5]

4. Luke 2:51.
5. Luke 14:26.

Here Jesus is issuing a call to follow him yet framing the cost of that apprenticeship in the starkest possible terms. That cost is none other than the detachment or loosening of familial relationships at such a deep level that it feels like hatred. Jesus is not, of course, advocating that one adopts a posture of hatred towards one's own family. He is deploying hyperbole in order to make a point. And that point is that the patterns of family relationships that one has known must now be examined and exposed for what they are. If there are attachments that are hindering the daring choice to follow Christ then they will be challenged.

The difficulty that many of us face, however, in following the path of transformation is that all too often our own attachment histories are far from being secure and healthy. The three other forms of adult attachment each carry with them associated responses to the prospect and the challenge of change. If the basic life orientation is imbued with high levels of anxiety or fearfulness, this will unavoidably determine how one faces new challenges, how one takes risks, and how the world itself is perceived. Many people know what it is to experience anxious-preoccupied relationships with our parents. In such environments a child can grow up imbibing the anxiety-based culture of the home and consider that to be normal. Those who grow up in homes in which relationships are characterized by anxious-preoccupied attachments can produce individuals who in later life develop a range of coping strategies that mask the deeply rooted fears that they have imbibed. Children growing up with a highly anxious parent may find themselves feeling responsible for that parent at a very young age, a state of affairs that is potentially highly toxic. If the parent is continually preoccupied or distracted, the child may easily begin to feel invisible, unnoticed, and easily forgotten. When the nature of the parental attachment is characterized by anxiety the effect on the child is to doubt the absolute security of that bond. An element of conditionality enters the parent–child dynamic so that the child might feel the need to constantly prove that he or she is worthy of parental love and affirmation. The seeds of performance-driven perfectionism lie here and it is maybe no surprise therefore to find adults who still feel the urgent need to win the approval of an aging parent. It is this longing for secure parental attachment, sought through achievement or obedience to the assumed values of the parental home that continues to drive behavior and choices. The call to follow Christ and to make this relationship primary inevitably brings such people into a collision course with the earlier attachment patterns.

Those with a dismissive-avoidant pattern of adult attachment may come across as highly resistant to any form of personal internal enquiry. Relationships in the home that are dismissive-avoidant can result in children who grow up feeling that they are unimportant. Cynicism has its roots in these homes, where newness, innovation, creativity, and risk-taking can be tossed aside with a quip or a put down. Homes characterized by dismissive-avoidant patterns of attachment generally do not deal very well with conflict or expressions of emotional vulnerability. There may be the denial of any need for greater social contact and a minimizing of the genuine social and emotional needs of others. The pattern observed by a child in these environments is one in which issues are not dealt with, where adults withdraw rather than converse, where emotions are hidden rather than exposed. It is an unsafe environment, where the home is no longer a haven from the pressures and stresses of the world but a place in which one has to remain on guard, wary of the next dismissive comment.

Fearful-avoidant patterns of attachment differ from dismissive-avoidant patterns in that those who exhibit significant levels of fear usually have a low view of themselves, undeserving of the love and support of others. This in turn means that there may well be an avoidance of intimacy and a pattern of forming short-term relationships in later life, which end when the fear of becoming too close becomes intolerable. The fear is that by forming an intimate attachment to someone there is the risk of later rejection and loss, a pattern that they once experienced from their parent at an early age. Those who have experienced homes marked by this type of attachment style may find it especially difficult to place trust in a living God who has promised not to reject them.

It is unlikely that many of us emerge into adulthood un-
scathed. We live in a world that is deeply resistant to the call of
God. It is a world scarred by violence, intolerance, and abuse. In
theological language, it is a world that has repeatedly turned away
from the God of love and fallen away from grace. And into our
own private worlds, which have been shaped by the attachments
we have grown up with, comes the call of Christ to follow him and
experience life in all its fullness. How we hear that call and respond
to it depends on how that voice is filtered through our own defense
mechanisms and preconceptions. What is an utterance of pure
love—*Come, follow me!*—can easily be heard in a myriad of different ways. It can be perceived as the voice of control or the voice
of manipulation. It can even sound foolish—who is issuing such a
strange request? Or it could be seen as a high risk venture—where
will such a call take me? The work of the Holy Spirit of grace is to
expose these defenses and bring them out into the open, where
they can be seen for what they are.

In conversation with Alison (introduced to us in chapter 1)
she explained that there had been significant signs of transformation in her life in recent years. When asked to offer an explanation
for this, her reply was perceptive and unsparingly honest. Alison
had grown up in a highly committed church-going family within
what could be described as the Pietist tradition. This meant family and personal devotions were a high priority, combined with
a wariness about worldly matters. There was a rigidity about the
family moral codes with a rather large list of prohibited activities
and attitudes. As Alison matured into adulthood and moved away
from the family home, the geographical distance gave her space
and time to reflect on her upbringing. Gradually she came to the
point of making a conscious choice. "I decided that I did not want
to grow up and become like my mother," she said. Her mother had
become for Alison an example of the kind of person she did not
want to become; someone who was, in her opinion, judgmental
of others, slightly prickly, disapproving, and fearful of the wider
world. Her revealing phrase "I did not want to be like my mother"
was indicative of an attachment issue that she was wrestling with.

The Pietist culture was characterized by an avoidant attitude to the world and a dismissive attitude to those who did not share this worldview. Over time Alison began to perceive this tradition as a potential breeding ground for an ugliness of character and she chose to distance herself from it. The gradual loosening of her loyalty to the family tradition demanded a radical re-think of what it meant to call herself a follower of Christ. This loosening of her familial attachments turned around the question of loyalty. If she no longer conformed to the family norms, would this be interpreted as disloyalty or, worse still, betrayal? Could she remain loyal to the family and especially to her mother, yet also choose her own personal distinctive mode of Christian discipleship? These questions took some years to resolve and Alison was only able to move forward once she had given herself sufficient internal permission to reframe the attachment to her mother in what she would now describe as a more mature, less childish manner.

A similar view was expressed by Mary who remarked that she had noticed a significant shift in herself over the years. She writes:

> I do have a more grace-filled perception of God nowadays, but I'm wondering if it is because I am older, with more experience of life, less rigid in my views, and therefore more forgiving? Or is it because, over the years I have listened to a lot of inflexible views which can be very critical and I don't want to be like those people!

In both of these stories the transformation that occurred was a result of a conscious negative choice. It was a decision to loosen the attachment with a particular person (Alison's mother) or tradition (Pietism) or, in Mary's case, with a particular group of people with whom she had been associated since her childhood.

The call to follow Christ is an invitation to assent to the process of transformation. It sounds simple enough, yet it requires the wisdom and skill to tread the tricky path between the injunction heard from the slopes of Mount Sinai in Exodus 20 to "honor your father and mother" and the words of Jesus to "hate your own father and mother." The Hebrew word translated as *honor* can also mean *glory*. It carries with it the sense of something weighty or heavy, something therefore of great value. To honor one's parents is to ensure that they are never belittled or brought into a place of shame and humiliation. It is to afford the highest respect to their intrinsic worth and dignity simply because they bear the image and likeness of God and gave us the gift of life. The sensitivity that exists around the issue of honoring one's parents is that *honor* and its opposite, *shame*, are often determined through cultural norms and reference.

Somewhere between these two poles of both honoring and leaving one's parents in the tangled and intimate web of relationships that we have with our parents is the road we are called to follow. It is a road filled with potholes and diversions and the capacity for self-deception is profoundly real. What may look like radical obedience to Christ may, at a deeper level, be simply the desire to please a father figure and to win his approval. Deep resistance to growth and transformation may have at its root the fear of causing distress to an aging mother figure. The call to discipleship and our own often complicated ties with our parents are intimately connected.

Sarah speaks of the effect of growing up with what she described as her *narcissistic mother*. Although she had been a Christian for many years she became increasingly dissatisfied with who she was. During a period of her adult life that afforded her long periods on her own she reflected on how her life had unfolded. She was able to describe an underlying rage that never truly dissipated combined with an urgent desire to be special. For her, "special" meant having the most expensive material goods and always having to be top of the class. She paints a picture of her life as one that was driven to succeed and to perform, yet always accompanied by a deep rooted anger. Her acute discomfort with who she had become drove her to re-examine her relationship with her mother. What she gradually came to realize is that her relationship with her mother was far from healthy or secure. Rather, she had spent her life anxiously trying to be different, to be better, such that she could be seen by her mother. Only when she was sufficiently special would her mother take any notice of her—at least that was how she perceived the nature of her attachment to her mother. This kind of attachment was conditional upon performance and resulted in the paradox of simultaneously being anxious to please her mother as well as raging against her.

Once she had come to this realization, she actively and consciously chose to let go of the hopes and expectations that she had nurtured all her life. These were longings to be seen and loved without the need to achieve or perform. She came to accept that her mother was unable to provide the kind of unconditional acceptance and warmth that Sarah craved and in that process of letting go Sarah experienced a huge sense of relief. Now she could be more true to herself, more authentic, and quite simply, in her own words, "more ordinary." For Sarah, the road to transformation was found in loosening her unhealthy attachment to her mother and finding a far deeper attachment in God. She even described God as her therapist. The key to unlocking the process of change for Sarah was discovering within herself the internal permission to leave her mother.

Sarah's depiction of God as her therapist reveals a new and deeper sense of spiritual attachment. Although she never used the language of the fatherhood or the motherhood of God, it is to this that she referred. Christ's instruction to his disciples when asked how to pray was to direct them towards God as Father. The apostle Paul's depiction of intimacy is framed in terms of *abba*, the Aramaic word for Daddy. The spirituality of Christian transformation lies within the family metaphor of parent and child relationships. All other depictions of God—Lord, Master, Creator, Sovereign—are not adequate to describe the depth of intimacy that is contained in the word Father.

This New Testament depiction of God was not entirely new. That most intimate of prayer books, the Psalms, contains hints at least that God can be understood as a Father. There are only a few psalms that use such a designation.

A father to the fatherless, a defender of widows, is God in his holy dwelling. [6]

He will call out to me, "You are my Father, my God, the Rock my Savior."[7]

As a father has compassion on his children, so the LORD has compassion on those who fear him.[8]

The beautiful Psalm 131 stands almost alone in using a maternal metaphor for God

> O Lord, my heart is not lifted up;
>   my eyes are not raised too high;
> I do not occupy myself with things
>   too great and too marvelous for me.
> But I have calmed and quieted my soul,
>   like a weaned child with its mother;
> like a weaned child is my soul within me.

Here we are left with an image of a young child who lies cradled in the arms of her mother, comforted, secure, and still. God is the mother of our souls in this psalm, the one who lifts us on to her lap and wraps her arms around us and stills the turmoil within each of us. It is as if the Motherhood and Fatherhood of God is an emerging, embryonic idea in the Old Testament that reaches its fullest and most complete expression in the coming of Jesus. This is why Jesus refers to the temple in Jerusalem as "my Father's house" when anxiously quizzed concerning his whereabouts by Mary and Joseph. And much later in his ministry, when Jesus gazes down upon the stubborn and rebellious city, he uses a female, maternal image to depict who he is:

> O Jerusalem, Jerusalem, the city that kills the prophets and stones those who are sent to it! How often would I have gathered your children together as a hen gathers her brood under her wings, and you were not willing![9]

6. Ps 68:5.
7. Ps 89:26.
8. Ps 103:13.
9. Luke 13:34.

These are essentially intimate terms expressing God's eternal commitment to us; a commitment that is unshakeable, secure, and unconditionally loving. It is as if all other terms for God find their culmination and fullest exposition in the one word Father. It is in the embrace of the Father that we know who we are and where we belong. Yet it is this very habitat that brings into question the kind of relationship that we have with our earthly father and, of course, our earthly mother too. The way in which we perceive the Fatherhood of God can be—and often is—filtered through the experiences that we have had with our own fathers. In the writings of the apostle Paul, the dominant metaphor used as a description of the nature and character of God is the term Father. In his pastoral letters this descriptor is used fifty-four times, a clear indication that his theology was imbued with the notion that the primary attribute of God is benevolence. Some theologies of salvation begin with God's justice and wrath and the need to establish a judicial basis on which to engage with vulnerable, broken humanity. The danger with such an approach is that the fatherhood of God becomes a secondary attribute, one that we only encounter once we have first been confronted with the God of retributive justice. If, however, God is understood to be Father from the first word until the last, then this suggests that the pressing need for humankind is a restoration, healing, and renewal of that most existential attachment of all, our earliest connection with our care givers. The fatherhood of God is not, therefore, revealed as a reward for those who have repented and believed; it is the way in which God is always to be perceived. When this kind of relational intimacy is experienced it offers a radically new, secure attachment, to return to Bowlby's categories, from which genuine and authentic transformation may take root.

John describes how he struggled for months to confront the issue of his own troubled relationship with his father, now long since dead. During a period of his life in which John had found any form of prayer immensely difficult, he sought out a spiritual director in the hope of obtaining some clarity about his confusion. His spiritual director had suggested to him that he simply use the Lord's Prayer each day, prayed slowly, savoring each word and phrase. After one month John returned to his director and explained that he was stuck, unable to get past the second word. That word, of course, was *Father*. Whenever he tried to use the prayer, the phrase "Our Father" stuck in his throat. For him it did not convey intimacy at all, but rather the opposite. The word Father spoke of harsh absenteeism, someone who was simply not there, not present, or if he was physically present then it was a cold judgmentalism. How could John use that term—Father—and address it to God? Over the ensuing months John gradually explored his relationship with his earthly father and came to see how this had given rise to such a significant distortion upon his own perception of God as Father. It was only through a process of letting go of an unhealthy attachment to his earthly father that he was able to reform and reconstruct an authentic depth to this attachment to his heavenly Father.

Bowlby's work on attachment was never intended to be used to understand spiritual dynamics of Christian discipleship. It was developed in order to provide a tool for describing the way in which early attachment patterns shape who we become in later life. It is these very patterns that remain lodged within each of us and with which we are confronted each time we hear the call to Christian transformation. How we negotiate the delicate path between hating our parents and honoring them exerts a huge influence in determining our own path of discipleship.

2

Discomfort

ONE OF THE MOST persistent themes to emerge in the interviews that were undertaken was that the catalyst that sparked the journey towards transformation was the pervasive, intrusive, unavoidable, presence of discomfort. It was by stepping into this darker avenue of pain, confusion, and suffering that the necessity to seek transformation acquired a new urgency. The discomfort became so loud that it demanded to be heard, which, in turn, required a re-ordering of the hitherto settled priorities in life. This unwelcome visitor named Pain came and encamped in the front room of the lives of those who told their stories, insisting on being listened to. The task that presented itself thus became clear: to find a way of developing a relationship with pain that allowed it to yield its rich fruits. Our guide into this world of discomfort is C. S. Lewis, one time Professor of English Literature at Oxford University and best known as the author of the Narnia Chronicles. Yet he was also an acute philosopher, theologian, and incisive observer of the human condition. His book, *The Problem of Pain*, published in 1940, has become over the years a Christian classic, for it is a philosophical exploration of the existence of evil and the role it plays in our lives. It is not my intention here to discuss the origin of evil or the thorny issue of theodicy. Rather, it is to assert that transformation into the likeness of Christ is *always* by way of discomfort. One of Lewis's most memorable quotations, found in his book is this:

> Pain insists on being attended to. God whispers to us in
> our pleasures, speaks in our conscience, but shouts in
> our pains; it is his megaphone to arouse a deaf world.[1]

Pain may feel like an unwelcome intruder into our lives. We may insist that pain is unfair, undeserved, uncalled for, and unnecessary, yet it persists and must somehow be negotiated, or, as Lewis has written, "attended to." Pain stops us in our tracks and compels us to rethink, to reconsider and to reflect on the nature of the course of our lives. When we walk down the street with comfortable shoes on we scarcely know what we are wearing on our feet. If there is a stone in our shoe, however, we are forced to stop walking and take it out. This is how pain functions, by introducing a braking mechanism in our journey through life.

There are, of course, many variant species of pain. There is the pain that seems to come to us from without. An unexpected loss, the arrival of ill health, an accident or an injury; all of these can make their appearance in our lives without forewarning or any invitation from us. They are simply given to us and this discomfort can sometimes happen in the most uncomfortable and unpleasant manner. But there is also the pain that arises from within. This can be equally acute and just as devastating. It is the pain of feeling that we have failed to live up to our own standards or that we have caused hurt to someone that we love. Or it can be a more nameless dread, the experience of shame that tells that we simply have no right to be who we are. This kind of pain can be piercingly sharp or shapelessly deadening. It can fracture our souls and tear us apart from within. Those who know this kind of pain say that it is the worse kind of suffering because it so internal and so utterly invisible. How then can pain be described as a necessity in the process of transformation? Isn't God's longing for our wholeness and healing rather than this ugly brute that strides in where it isn't welcome?

C. S. Lewis wrote that "pain shatters the creature's false self-sufficiency."[2] This, it seems, is its vital function. Pain strips away the layers of false selves that are so easily constructed around our

1. Lewis, *The Problem of Pain*, 81.
2. Ibid., 90.

own fragility. Without pain it may be possible to live happily with our own self-delusions, self-justifications, and the masks that we wear. Once pain steps into our lives the dismantling of all that is false about us can truly begin. Michael, one of those interviewed, writes about his relationship with discomfort.

> Like most good addicts, I will medicate and do almost anything to avoid pain and discomfort. I'm human. I wish I wouldn't avoid pain. I think that because of pain avoidance I stayed in abusive situations too long. In my seeking transformation what provoked it was almost always crisis—which is another word for pain or discomfort. So as much as I try to avoid pain by running or medicating to get rid of it, I also know that pain is something very positive because it causes me to seek hope and healing. It triggers transformation. I now believe pain is a gift from God, even though I wish it would just go away. But I can see how often God has used it for major transformation.

C. S. Lewis echoes these same sentiments. Writing about his own experience of discomfort he honestly admits:

> I am a great coward. When I think of pain, of anxiety that gnaws like fire and loneliness that spreads out like a desert and the heartbreaking routine of monotonous misery, or again the dull aches that blacken our whole landscape or sudden nauseating pain that knocks a man's heart out at one blow, of pains that seem already intolerable and then are suddenly increased. . . . If I knew of any way of escape I would crawl through sewers to find it. . . . Pain hurts. To prove it palatable is beyond my design.[3]

The Psalmist too knew all about pain. Some of the most poignant psalms are those that deal with the painful experience of disorientation. Psalm 13 is a good example:

> For the director of music. A psalm of David.
> How long, LORD? Will you forget me forever?
> How long will you hide your face from me?
> How long must I wrestle with my thoughts

3. Ibid., 93.

and day after day have sorrow in my heart?
How long will my enemy triumph over me?
Look on me and answer, LORD my God.
Give light to my eyes, or I will sleep in death,
    and my enemy will say, "I have overcome him,"
    and my foes will rejoice when I fall.
But I trust in your unfailing love;
    my heart rejoices in your salvation.
I will sing the Lord's praise,
    for he has been good to me.

The writer, King David, is experiencing a particularly acute period of sorrow and chooses to pin the blame firmly where it belongs—on God. It is God who has let him down. He feels that God has abandoned him and hidden his face so that there is the terrifying experience of being utterly alone in a hostile world. For long days and nights he has wrestled with troubling, disturbing thoughts that are full of the accusatory taunts of those around him. His pain is compounded by the inability to sleep. The Old Testament commentator Walter Brueggemann writes that such psalms of darkness,

> may be judged by the world to be acts of unfaith and failure, but for the trusting community their use is an act of bold faith, albeit a transformed faith. . . . It is bold because it insists that all such experiences of disorder are a proper subject for discourse with God. There is nothing out of bounds, nothing precluded or inappropriate. Everything properly belongs in this conversation of the heart.[4]

It is precisely via means of this searingly honest engagement with God, made urgent because of acute discomfort, that the Psalmist eventually arrives at a place of re-orientation. Between the statement that his foes will rejoice when he falls and the radical announcement heralded by the word "but," there is a time of waiting. He has poured out his soul to God in lament and there is nothing more that can be added until the period of waiting is over. The

4. Brueggemann, *The Message of the Psalms,* 52.

waiting demands a trust that the world that God has made is not a place of perpetual disorientation and that God is finally able to cause hope to emerge from darkness. The "but" towards the end of the psalm announces that a shaft of light has entered David, a glimmer of renewed hope and signs of joy. Arriving at this place of transformed faith could only occur because of the journey through the vale of sadness expressed in the opening stanzas. One curious aspect of the psalm is that the writer does not demand that the pain is taken away. What he urgently longs for is the reassurance of knowing that the face of God has not turned away from him. If only he could experience once again the knowledge that God's face was orientated towards him, it would give "light to his eyes." He is asking poetically for a renewed perspective on his suffering rather than its removal. It is this kind of alternative relationship with suffering that Jessica Powers captures so beautifully in this poem

> All that day long I spent the hours with suffering.
> I woke to find her sitting by my bed.
> She stalked my footsteps while time slowed to timeless,
> tortured my sight, came close in what I said
> She asked me no more than that,
> beneath unwelcome,
> I might be mindful of her grant of grace.
> I still can smile, amused, when I remember
> how I surprised her when I kissed her face.[5]

The poet writes as if suffering is a person who demands to be heard. Suffering comes to us in the privacy of our own bedrooms and takes up residence there. She never leaves, even when we angrily demand that she goes at once, never to return. Suffering, when regarded as a useless, futile, spiky visitor to our lives has the capacity to make us bitter and resentful, especially when we attempt to wish it away or insist that it is unfairly and unjustly present. Such a stance only seems to give suffering greater resilience and staying power. While Psalm 13 is full of complaint and angry lament, the focus is not on the removal of suffering but on the need for presence, the presence of the wholly other to look together at the experience of

5. Kappes, *Track of the Mystic,* 111.

sadness. When we know the face of God compassionately gazing in our direction, the sting and the power of suffering are lessened. The Psalmist, over time, returns to the place of doxology, but the path to this place of shalom is strewn with discomfort.

The experience of the disciple Peter is illustrative of the role of discomfort in an entirely different context. For the Psalmist, the suffering seemed to be compounded by the taunting of his compatriots. For Peter, his suffering was entirely self-inflicted. Peter's confident assertion that he would always stick by the side of Jesus, through thick and thin, was put to the test at the moment of Jesus's arrest. His subsequent threefold denial of Jesus is poignantly recorded by Luke when he simply states "The Lord turned and looked straight at Peter."[6] Luke displays his masterly storytelling gifts in the devastating simplicity of this statement. It was the glance of recognition, searing in its quality and depth of penetration. Peter is exposed in a public place and all his bluff and bluster and protestations of fearless commitment to Christ evaporate in that one instant. It was a pivotal moment for Peter, bringing to light the fickleness of his own heart and the collapse of his character in the face of the first signs of danger. His discomfort was acute, provoking an existential crisis of being. It was not until some weeks later, in the aftermath of the resurrection on a lonely beach, that his rehabilitation was begun. There, in the breakfast encounter with the risen Christ, he once more faces the gaze of Christ over the embers of the fire. On this occasion Christ speaks to him with the same penetrating insights, the identical form of searching that exposed the truth about the state of Peter's heart.

> When they had finished eating, Jesus said to Simon Peter, "Simon son of John, do you love me more than these?" "Yes, Lord," he said, "you know that I love you." Jesus said, 'Feed my lambs."
>
> Again Jesus said, "Simon son of John, do you love me?" He answered, "Yes, Lord, you know that I love you." Jesus said, "Take care of my sheep."

6. Luke 22:16.

35

The third time he said to him, "Simon son of John, do you love me?" Peter was hurt because Jesus asked him the third time, "Do you love me?" He said, "Lord, you know all things; you know that I love you."[7]

Both stories about Peter, the glance at the time of trial and the more leisurely conversation on the shore, belong together. They deal with the moment when Peter felt the deep unbearable pain of failure and the subsequent opportunity to take this occasion and allow it to become the place of newness. In that one glance something in Peter died. In that later early morning meal something new was born.

C. S. Lewis understood well the vagaries of the human heart. He knew all about our cravings for an undisturbed, settled, secure life where all our anchorage points of security and significance are firmly in place. Yet he also realized that such safe places do not always enable us to grow for we can so easily deceive ourselves that this is our true resting place. He writes:

> The security we crave would teach us to rest our hearts in this world and oppose an obstacle to our return to God: a few moments of happy love, a landscape, a symphony, a merry meeting with our friends, a bathe or a football match, have no such tendency. Our Father refreshes us on our journey with some pleasant inns, but will not encourage us to mistake them for home.[8]

This is precisely the kind of epiphany that Lucy experienced. Lucy was one of those interviewed in the course of writing this book. Lucy had lived with her disabled sister for over thirty years, caring for her and giving herself to attend to her needs. Throughout this period Lucy had devoted her energies to this one task and when her sister suddenly died, a huge hole was left in Lucy's life. The painful experience of bereavement proved to be the catalyst for Lucy's journey towards transformation. This is how she reflected on the process.

---

7. John 21:15.

8. Lewis, *The Problem of Pain*, 103.

When my sister died I was suddenly faced with the question, how am I going to live now? What foundation had I built my life upon? Was any of it true? I went through a time of deep reflection. I looked back on the whole of my lifetime and looked at the choices I had made. Something like a major grief puts you on a windswept moor with nothing solid around you, nothing familiar and at that point you feel completely stripped. I realized I could not rescue myself from this grief; I couldn't do this on my own. When my sister was alive we were companions, we supported each other. In many ways we completely depended on one another, and now that she is gone it is just me on my own. Initially there was an overwhelming feeling of panic. What has changed since then however is not so much my theology but the place of my dependence. Before she died we depended on each other. Now that she is gone I have had to learn a more authentic way of being dependent on God. The lived experience of faith is now very different. It is not so much a different belief but rather a different way of believing.

Yet Lucy also knew that bereavement does not on its own, as if by some unconscious process, effect transformation. She had observed in her own mother how her grief had never truly been resolved, leaving her mother locked in a place of permanent, frozen mourning. Here is Lucy again in her own words:

When my father died my mother did not change anything whatsoever. She didn't do anything, she just wanted everything back the way it was and she lived for nine years like that until she died. I decided I didn't want to live like that. That was a motivator. I watched her exist for nine years with a permanent nostalgia. I decided I did not want to grieve like my mother.

The grief that Lucy endured through the loss of her sister had the effect of sharpening her own powers of observation. She noticed how grief had been dealt with within her family circle and how unproductive it had been. This observation gave her the resolve to approach her own grief differently, to explore it more fully and with greater honesty. When asked how this experience of profound loss had impacted her faith, Lucy replied:

> When everything that I had held dear for my entire life was ripped away from me and nothing was the same any more I found that the rope that connected me to God, which he was holding, was strong enough to hold me. The rope never slipped.

Lucy's story is one of the emergence of a deeper, truer faith as the outcome of suffering. Yet for many the burning question that needs to be addressed in the face of pain is framed around the issue of justice. Of course, it is not always articulated quite like that, but the struggle turns around the theme of whether our discomfort is deserved or undeserved. If we reckon that our present difficult circumstances are deserved it leads us on a relentless search to find and unearth the failings or misdemeanors that we might have committed. "If there is pain then it must be my fault," can be the default position of some unfortunate souls. It reveals an underlying theology that is thoroughly mechanical in that each and every sin and omission elicits an equal, painful, consequence sent from heaven above. Such a view of pain only serves to add further burdens on to the shoulders of those who are already suffering and does not lead towards a more wholesome, life-giving, transformed life.

An alternative response to pain—that it is completely undeserved and therefore thoroughly unfair—is equally troublesome. Such an attitude is combative, angry, prickly, and leaves little room for prayerful reflection. It can be detected in those who appear to have a victim mentality, often deferring to a fatalistic approach to the circumstances of life. "If there is a God," one might murmur internally, "then such gross miscarriages of justice would not happen." The problem with both of these responses to pain is the often-fruitless search for a cause. If only the origin of one's pain can be found then pain, surely, will cease. The reality of discomfort and the value that can be derived from it lies in neither of these responses. Both responses reveal a view of God that lurks behind the pain. If God is perceived to be utterly sovereign and omnipotent, then the fine details of each and every event that occur throughout creation are subject to his controlling power. Such an understanding of the way God interacts in our world may lead to the conclusion that God must be unjust, for pain, suffering, and discomfort never appear to be distributed fairly. Alternatively, if God is the one who is understood to be simply reacting to our human choices, meting out rewards and punishments according to deeds done or omitted, then God becomes merely the cosmic mathematician whose concern is merely to balance the books. There is, furthermore, a third perspective on God as the one who is not involved in the minutiae of our lives, detached, disinterested, at least one step removed from the painful intrusions into our lives.

The relationship that we form with pain is thus, at heart, a consequence of the way in which we perceive and experience God. The "problem of pain" as C. S. Lewis phrased it, is really the problem of God. Finding the hidden treasure that lies buried within discomfort is nothing more or less than finding God dwelling in that painful place too. This was the cry of Job's heart all along. Job's tale is well known. An upstanding member of the community, happily settled with a growing family dwelling on fruitful land, he was inexplicably struck down with a series of terrifying tragedies. Eventually he sits alone, having lost all that was dear to him, with his acute grief compounded by physical distress. His friends attempt to offer explanations and solace for this turn of events, but to no avail. In the midst of the most acute suffering, Job longed to see afresh where God could be found. The answer that came after thirty-eight chapters of tortured agonizing was really no answer at all. God's voice to Job was to confront him with awe—the awesomeness of creation itself.

> Where were you when I laid the earth's foundation? Tell me, if you understand. Who marked off its dimensions? Surely you know! Who stretched a measuring line across it? On what were its footings set, or who laid its cornerstone—while the morning stars sang together and all the angels shouted for joy?[9]

9. Job 38:4.

God speaks in mystical poetry, hurling images and metaphors at Job until he is overwhelmed by the majesty of the sublime. God is the Creator and Sustainer of all that is, his voice declares, but not in the crude mechanical, mathematical way that some may perceive him. God is present in the suffering of humanity—of course! But not in the simplistic, superficial, fairy godmother sense. Job's tortured questions about his own suffering melted away once he had heard God's voice to him.

Coming face to face with the sheer magnitude, dynamism, and beauty of creation was something that consumed the intellect of the great Enlightenment philosopher Emmanuel Kant. His energies had been devoted to establishing a secure and indeed pre-eminent place for human rationality. He applied his immense mind to the tricky questions of ethical imperatives, the nature and purpose of aesthetics, and the role of the divine in human endeavor. He employed the notion of God because of its usefulness for underpinning ethical living, in that the divine possessed the function of providing a yardstick or an impetus for moral behavior. Yet he was confounded by the experience of what he termed "the sublime." What happens to humanity when confronted with the sublime? What is the range of responses to the terrifying, overwhelming forces of nature? The sublime plumbs the depths and soars to the heights of what the imagination is capable of perceiving. It provokes the imagination to enter strange new territory; the land of super abundance. The sublime can produce reactions of terror or quiet wonder or nobility. The experience of being in the presence of the sublime, Kant observed, only leads to awe, and awe is beyond the reach of human rationality and explanation.

"There is a paradox about tribulation in Christianity,"[10] observed C. S. Lewis. On the one hand, it is often via means of pain that we are brought into a fresh experience of the immanence of the God who dwells among us, even in the most acute forms of suffering. Yet pain in itself is not something intrinsically good that we must embrace stoically, knowing it is supposedly beneficial for our souls. We have no need to masochistically look for suffering

10. Lewis, C.S. *The Problem of Pain*, 98.

in order to be made into whole people. The healing ministry of Jesus is testament to the yearning compassion of God who seeks to bring healing from distress and disability. The paradox lies in holding together—simultaneously—the legitimate desire for pain and discomfort to be removed by God whilst knowing that it is here, in these dark places, that God may be found in ways that are simply not possible when life is too comfortable. The search for God's balm in the midst of suffering whilst at the same time allowing suffering to do its work within us, lies at the heart of this curious yet beautiful journey towards transformation.

3

Narrative

NARRATIVES—OR STORIES—FASCINATE US. TRY eavesdropping on a conversation between friends on a bus and notice how the speech is usually an interweaving of shared stories, peppered with anecdotes. We meet one another and ask each other how our day has been, how our relationships are faring, and what experiences we have had. All of this is couched in the form of story, and it is as we tell one another our stories that we disclose something of ourselves. It is as we listen to the stories of others that we build up a picture of who is facing us, for without stories there would be little meaning in our lives. The curious thing about the stories we tell about ourselves is that they possess the power both to transform as well as to entrap. Our narratives are woven from the disparate events, experiences, and relationships in our lives to form a tapestry that depicts who we are. Once the weaving process has been completed, it is commonplace to inhabit the world that has been created, believing it to be the truth, the whole truth, and nothing but the truth about who we are. Yet stories are, in reality, not nearly so rigid. They are supple, open to re-telling, and it is at this point that the story of Christ entering our world and thus entering our lives has the potential to usher in something utterly new and transformative.

One key thinker in the twentieth century who explored how narratives function in the development of our sense of identity is the French philosopher Paul Ricoeur. From the outset of his career

Ricoeur was engaged in a constant search to articulate what it means to be human. In what is probably his most significant publication, *Time and Narrative*, Ricoeur attempted to explore what it means to be a human-being-in-time. He does so in response to the great North African theologian St. Augustine, who in his *Confessions*, written in the late fourth century, posed the fundamental philosophical problem of establishing how we are related to time. "How can time exist," asked Augustine, "if the past is no longer there, the future is not yet, and the present passes away?" Ricoeur takes up this challenge and in so doing he asserts that there are two distinct types of time. The first is *chronological time* in which a sequence of events succeed one another in a uniform, linear way. The second is *episodic time*, referring to moments of significance that stand out in the memory. Ricoeur attempted to find a way of connecting these two. He proposed a third form of time, which he named *narrated time*, bridging the gap between the two poles. It is through narrated time that the episodic and the chronological aspects of time intersect and inhabit one another. Narratives describe the moments in time when we as humans can be both the cause of actions and the recipients of actions performed by others.

The distinguishing mark of narrated time is that it has to be configured. Most of us are familiar with the term configuration in connection with installing a computer or observing a piece of art. Configuration refers to the way in which the different parts of a machine are assembled, or the way in which the various actors in a play interact, and, in the case of stories, how we join together the various experiences of our lives to form a narrative. Narrative configuration is the art of assembling a tale about ourselves, which involves selecting the individual stories of our lives and weaving them together to form a plot. Obviously we cannot tell absolutely everything that there is to tell, so this process of configuring involves not only remembering and selecting from our store of experiences but simultaneously forgetting and de-selecting other events that we do not wish to include. The process of selecting, rejecting, and weaving together is what Ricoeur referred to as "emplotment." Emplotment is Ricoeur's technical term for the construction of a narrative that is intended to elicit a particular meaning. In practice, it is not dissimilar to the childhood game of joining up the dots to create a picture. How we join up the dots, each of which is a story in itself, depends on the meaning we wish to create for ourselves or for the benefit of our listeners.

Ricoeur claimed that humanity is on a relentless search for meaning, which we find in the stories that we tell about ourselves or in the stories that we read. As such, we find huge significance in symbols, myths, metaphor, poetry, and history, all of which are disparate styles of storytelling. Ricoeur's theory of narrative is a useful starting point in our examination of how our minds work in a narrative manner. His concern was to find what he termed a "narrative theology," which sought to construct meaning out of "the intersection between the world of the text and the world of the reader."[1] What he meant by this was that when we read the pages of Scripture we come face-to-face with stories about events that took place many centuries ago, stories that make claims about the activity of God and the person of Christ. We come to those sacred texts with the narratives of our own lives lodged in our consciousness and, it must be stressed, lodged within our unconsciousness too. Here two different narrative worlds meet each other and between two worlds meaning can be constructed about who we are, the trajectory that our lives are taking, and the reality of God in our lives. The process of negotiating the intersection between these two worlds is the task that each of us faces. Either we keep the two worlds separate and distinct without allowing them to speak to one another or we initiate a narrative dialogue, a dialogue that has the potential to transform. If we stand back and observe ourselves as we face a new situation, we may be able to resonate with the following sequence of events.

1. Ricoeur, *Figuring the Sacred*, 240.

STAGE ONE

Something happens. It may be a chance encounter with someone, it may be the news that we have been unsuccessful in a job application, or we have fallen ill, or fallen in love, or a million and one other possibilities. We experience an emotion concerning this event. This emotion may evoke memories, it may produce fear, irritation, joy, anxiety, elation.

STAGE TWO

We search for similarities or connections with previous emotional reactions. When did this happen before? Why am I feeling like this? Does this event fit in with an observable pattern in my life? We join together this current event with previous similar events and ascribe an intention (if the event involved a person) or a motive or a purpose or a particular meaning. We may search for examples in our own history that confirm the validity and authenticity of the story that we have just created.

STAGE THREE

The story becomes solidified such that it is unquestioned and regarded as completely true, and in the light of the story that we have shaped, our behavior and choices are determined.

All of this can happen in less than a second! Our story is a reality that exists only in our minds; it is our personal, private construction. The astonishing thing about our narratives is just how resilient they are. If we have been telling ourselves the same stories all of our lives then it is simply instinctive to allocate each new experience as an additional chapter in an already existing plot. It is only when the new experience is so dissonant, so uncomfortable, so utterly odd, that we are compelled to revisit our narratives and begin the excruciating process of deconstruction. This process of tearing down in order to rebuild is part of the process of renewing the mind.

So how does this deconstruction process take place? How does a new story emerge that resonates more closely not only with the reality of my own experience, but also with a greater faithfulness to the story of the gospel itself? My proposal takes a similar path to the one outlined above.

STAGE ONE

There is an experience of radical newness. This new event could be profoundly painful, producing a deeply uncomfortable or stressful feeling. Something is wrong here! Something is not working, something does not fit in with my expectations. Alternatively, the new event may be so unexpectedly beautiful, with a hint of the sacred perhaps, a touch of the Holy Spirit, inspiring awe such that we simply do not possess any categories in our mental filing system to cope with it.

STAGE TWO

There is often the acknowledgement that we wish reality was different. This reality does not suit me! We may find ourselves at war with the world and therefore at war with ourselves. If the new reality is unreservedly wonderful we are aware that there is now a huge gap between our expectations of what ought to be and the reality of what is.

STAGE THREE

A growing need arises within us for something or someone external to us to reflect back the story that we have constructed. This may produce a realization that the reality that we have constructed thus far is not working. It can produce stress and anxiety for the need to tear down the narrative home that we have built for ourselves has become progressively more apparent. It can also elicit elation. At long last! We can see how myopic we may have been!

It is now possible that we can see with new eyes the presence and activity of God where before we had presumed otherwise.

STAGE FOUR

We begin to feel the need to construct a counter story that has greater resonance with reality. Gradually there arises a growing list of reasons to let go of the story that we have believed for so long. We make a decision, consciously or unconsciously, to inhabit a different story that has greater resonance with reality. The new narrative brings with it an emotional reaction that is comforting.

In contrast to the first set of stages, this process of replacing one narrative with another can be long, slow, incremental, and deeply unsettling. It is, however, ultimately profoundly liberating. The Christian call to discipleship is none other than the call to inhabit a brand new story that leads towards life in all its abundance. Let us now examine the story of Paul in the light of this model of narrative reconstruction.

By his own admission, Paul inhabited an apparently secure story. Born into the tribe of Benjamin, a thoroughgoing Hebrew, educated into the tradition of the Torah, a teacher, a leader, an enforcer. By his own admission, the narrative of his life was blameless. He had experienced no sense of doubt or unease, there was no sign of any growing conviction that his life of faith was in any way deficient. Furthermore, his narrative could be traced back thousands of years to the patriarchs of the Old Testament and it was within this flow of history that he found his place. Yet the irruption of this new Christian sect into his comfortably defined world was deeply disturbing. In his opinion it was merely an irritation and a potentially dangerous one at that. This sect had rapidly gained new adherents and won the favor of the population with surprising speed. Paul experienced a deeply uncomfortable dislocation.

One member of this new sect, a man called Stephen, was called to account one day,[2] yet displayed such courage, such faith,

---

2. Acts 7.

such brazen fearlessness in the face of intense interrogation and threats that Paul wholeheartedly supported his public execution. Stephen was a man of good deeds—gracious, kind, gentle, popular, and generous. But the role that Stephen played as a distributor of alms to the poor and his godly personal demeanor simply did not fit into the narrative of Paul's life. There was no question that this man, this disturber, must die. In the mind of Paul, Stephen was a threat to Paul's existence as a leader of the Pharisees, and he was determined to defend and protect the tradition into which he had been born.

In order to complete his desire to purge his nation of this new sect he journeys towards the city of Damascus. On this journey Paul experiences a radical interruption, an experience of complete disorientation through an encounter with the risen Christ. The focal point of this encounter is the conversation that takes place between Paul and Christ in the aftermath of Paul's fall to the ground. Christ holds a mirror up to Paul and explains that his persecution of the Christian sect is nothing less than the persecution of Christ too. Christ reflects back to Paul his own behavior, and in so doing offers an entirely new interpretation. In effect Christ re-configured the narrative of Paul's life. Paul realized that when he thought that he was defending God from the dangers of the Christian sect he was in reality at war with God in the person of his son Jesus Christ. His previous narrative now appears to have no validity at all.

Some years later Paul reflected on this moment in the story of his life and described it in the opening chapter of his letter to the Galatians. Paul observes that in that moment of encounter on the Damascus road two processes were taking place simultaneously. One was the immediate renunciation of the narrative of being "extremely zealous for the traditions of my fathers" (Gal 1:14). This had been his story for many years, yet in that one instant of epiphany the narrative was jettisoned. Secondly, there was the acceptance of a new narrative now defined in terms of calling or vocation. The encounter with Christ is now seen as the *kairos* moment of the annunciation of his call. In fact, this vocation, Paul now admits in his letter, had been in place from his birth, yet it had been unrecognized and unacknowledged.

Paul's response to the call of Christ was to submit himself to the care and the authority of the fledgling Christian community. He allows himself to be led by the hand to the city of Damascus and there to be introduced to Ananias who would himself become the instrument of Paul's healing. His habitation in an entirely new narrative signified a new sense of belonging within a community of faith that had not been part of his Pharisaic tradition. Within a short space of time Paul heeds the call of Christ to take the gospel story to the Gentiles and dares to take for himself the title of apostle. In this way, his own re-naming signaled the complete deconstruction of his previous narrative and his willing adoption of a new story. Paul realizes that this new identity is simply the discovery of his true identity given to him long ago.

Some years later Paul writes to the church in Philippi and describes a peace that is ineffable in the beautiful phrase "and the peace of God, which transcends all understanding, . . ." Paul now knows the experience of peace, yet this is a peace that is not explicable in ordinary categories. It is a peace that transcends cognition, which transcends emotion even. It is a participation in the life of God in the knowledge that Christ is not "out there," but that his own life is hidden with Christ himself. This is the new story of Paul and it is one that results in this sublime experience of peace. Paul has become who he truly is with his new identity secure and his old narrative of aggression and defensiveness having long since disappeared.

Paul's dramatic reconfiguration of the story of his life informed the way in which he dealt with pastoral situations in the churches that he founded. One of the most troubled communities was in Galatia, where a deep rift appeared between those Christ-believers from a Jewish background and Gentiles who had embraced the gospel. The contentious issue revolved around the role of the law and whether it continued to possess any binding legitimacy over those who did not come from a Jewish background. Paul addresses the issue by an appeal to narrative. His letter acknowledges that the Torah had played a central guiding function in the lives of the Jewish Christians. Their story began with Moses and the reception of the law in tablets of stone. For them the notion that this component of the narrative of their lives could be dispensed with was considered to be utterly impossible. The law was God-given and therefore it was forever. Paul points out that there is an alternative narrative sub-structure to the story of the Jewish people. He says that their narrative configuration is, in effect, truncated in that the story is too short. The story of faith does not begin with Moses but with Abraham some centuries earlier. It is Abraham, not Moses, who is the iconic model of faith. He is the one who had placed his trust in God long before any law had been given. The exercise of faith in response to the overtures of grace is demonstrated in the life of Abraham and thus faith is to be understood as a divine gift unconnected to either the giving or the reception of the law. To make such a daring claim was to lay oneself open to the charge of minimizing the enduring significance of the law. Paul could only take such a bold step in his argumentation by locating the story of the law within the larger story of God's dealing with the patriarch Abraham.

But the question still remained; if faith and law are unconnected, then what role does the law have? Paul anticipates this question by acknowledging that the law had played a crucial role in the unfolding narrative of the Jewish people, but only as an interim measure to prepare them for the coming of Christ who would be the fulfillment of the law. Once Christ has come the purpose of the law was completed and therefore had no abiding claim on the lives of those who now placed their trust in Christ. This way of telling the story ensured that the role and status of the law was re-framed. It was not to be despised, discarded, or ignored, but rather its pivotal, guiding role was reconfigured. Paul's pastoral approach is infused with narrative reconstruction. It was vital that the Christians from a Gentile background were not persuaded to adopt ancient Jewish practices; it was equally important that the troublesome Judaizers came to see that their narrative, which revolved around Torah observance, was replaced by the new Christ-centered story

This narrative approach to the transformation of a church has many obvious resonances with a whole range of contemporary situations. On a corporate level, the narrative of a community is a shared one that emerges over time and is often defined by key defining moments that function as a reference point. Such moments could be the day a victory was won, the time when a bomb exploded, or the occasion when a significant figure achieved something of huge importance. These points in time become incorporated into the story of group of people, shaping who they are and how they view themselves. Each November in the United Kingdom the Remembrance Day commemorations retell the stories of suffering, heroism, and bravery contained in Britain's numerous military engagements over the past 100 years. The way in which these stories are told is done with sensitivity, avoiding any jingoistic triumphalism but emphasizing the human cost of warfare. This annual tradition has become part of the narrative identity of the nation and, one might argue, serves a noble purpose.

Not all corporate storytelling is so noble, however. It is entirely possible for churches to tell their own stories in terms that glorify a particular time in history that has now been lost or in terms of defining themselves against a perceived enemy. Such storytelling merely serves to encase a community in protective walls and perhaps preserve a victim identity. Psalm 137 is just such a tale articulating a collectively owned narrative.

> By the rivers of Babylon we sat and wept when we remembered Zion. There on the poplars we hung our harps, for there our captors asked us for songs, our tormentors demanded songs of joy; they said, "Sing us one of the songs of Zion!" How can we sing the songs of the Lord while in a foreign land?

The psalm tells a story that connects together the memory of home with the daily experience of humiliation. It paints a picture of a group of displaced, dishonored people encamped against their will beside a river in a foreign land. Surrounding them are the powerful captors who torment them each day, mocking their impoverished existence. This is the narrative of hopelessness and despair, the story of unremitting loss, rendering those who tell the story as victims. This is their narrative in which they dwell. The danger for this community of exiles was that a rigid narrative of corporate loss would only serve to ensure that a closed mentality is perpetuated. Once this stage is reached the community begin to tell their corporate story in terms of their final, irreversible abandonment by God. It was a danger that the prophets immediately recognized, impelling them to step into these narratives and to dramatically present an alternative narrative of hope. Ezekiel comes forward and declares:

> Then he said to me: "Son of man, these bones are the people of Israel. They say, 'Our bones are dried up and our hope is gone; we are cut off.' Therefore prophesy and say to them: 'This is what the Sovereign LORD says: My people, I am going to open your graves and bring you up from them; I will bring you back to the land of Israel. Then you, my people, will know that I am the LORD, when I open your graves and bring you up from them. I will put my Spirit in you and you will live, and I will settle you in your own land. Then you will know that I the LORD have spoken, and I have done it, declares the LORD.'"[3]

Ezekiel deploys the powerful language of metaphor woven into a brand new tale. Ricoeur was fascinated with metaphor and symbol, claiming that such forms of speech create "an overflow of possibilities." It was by means of metaphor that the rich, fecund language of new narratives can be imagined and inhabited. For Ricoeur, fresh metaphors reveal a new way of seeing what is referred to. Metaphors take language and transform it creatively, thereby producing new meanings. Ezekiel knew the depth of pain that the exiled Jewish community were enduring. He understood that their experience of exile was akin to a death whereby nothing remains except bones and graves. This is the emotional and spiritual land in which they dwell, a place where all hope has been extinguished. Ezekiel takes their own metaphors—bones and graves—and transforms them by placing them in a new story in

3. Ezek 37:11–14

which the impossible becomes possible, death is turned into life and absence becomes homecoming. It is a powerfully attractive new narrative uttered with the authoritative force of "this is the word of the LORD," demanding that it be heard with the utmost seriousness. The story that Ezekiel tells depicts the LORD as the one central character who is engaged in a surprising, astonishing activity. The LORD goes to the place of death and there he will open up graves and will personally transport his people back to a fertile and plentiful land. The LORD is depicted in terms which defy their perceptions. This is not a God who is inactive or who has forgotten and abandoned his people. No! He is a God who is continually on the search to bring the new shoots of life out of seemingly impossible, hopeless situations. This is the power of a narrative re-telling of the story of exile.

Yet narratives are not only corporately owned. We each construct our own stories from the fragments of our lives, searching constantly to create meaning by plotting a path through the muddle. It is not uncommon for those individuals who have suffered a trauma of some kind, for example, to find that a traumatic event, or a sequence of traumatic events, forms the predominant cornerstone of the story of their lives. The trauma becomes the story of who they are and the danger is that such a narrative can lock people into a lifelong victim identity. In Northern Ireland, where I now live, there are many people still haunted by their own tragic stories of "the troubles," in which tales of lost loved ones define and shape the story of their lives. Is there a way in which these stories of acute and searing loss can be transformed into something beautiful and whole? Could the narrative of those who have suffered be re-framed or re-configured in such a way as to include the story of Christ at each stage of the unfolding tale? What would happen to the narrative of loss if the story was re-told in an alternative way, beginning perhaps at a different starting point, deselecting some elements of the narrative and emphasizing others? Such an exercise is not an attempt to fool oneself but to allow an alternative story to be told that is just as true, but perhaps more life-giving and life-affirming. A Christian approach to narrative transformation is not un-boundaried but is contained with the framework of the narratives that Scripture itself offers us. Whilst we may not have suffered the pain of exile in a foreign land like those depicted in Psalm 137, we may be able to imaginatively place ourselves within their story of exile and loss and from within that biblical story make it our own. The words of Ezekiel offering hope and empowerment may then be heard with fresh ears.

When asked to tell the story of his life five years ago and the story of his life now, Michael wrote the following.

> Some years ago, I was like a little child trying so very hard to gain God's approval. I remember having a childhood fantasy, where I had a beloved favorite teacher. I would fantasize that I actually had a relationship with her—that she cared about me. And then I was never good enough, and she would punish me for my inadequacy. Here is the one I so want to please, and I can't do it. I'm insufficient. I think that I could still see God as that teacher who would punish me for not being good enough. So a primary narrative set of words would include inadequate, failure, not good enough, displeasing, back sliding, sinful so that I couldn't even be in God's presence, not making the grade. I don't actually think that God was punishing me; I just think that I saw God as being pretty appalled by me. What is happening more recently is that that story has faded away and now I am getting used to a new story, one in which God is holding my gaze and I am holding God's gaze—and me encountering a God who really rejoices in me and our relationship. It is so different from what I've been taught or used to.

The shift that had occurred for Michael was depicted in terms of a recurrent tale of fearful inadequacy before a God who was once viewed as a particularly pedantic schoolteacher and the present day story of a God who now looked with delight at Michael regardless of his achievements. The new narrative has the ring of liberation about it similar to the fresh hopefulness of Ezekiel's prophetic utterances many hundreds of years earlier.

Telling the story of our lives is never an objective factual exercise. Whilst we may not always be able to control the circumstances and events of our lives, the way in which the narrative trajectory of who we are is told, is fluid, dynamic, and open to endless re-tellings. The road towards Christian transformation invites such re-tellings in the light of new epiphanies experienced, or out of an urgent need to be liberated from a story that has encased us for too long. The paradigmatic story of Mary and her encounter with the angel Gabriel referred to in the introductory chapter, resulted in a brand new story, the song of Mary.

> My soul glorifies the Lord and my spirit rejoices in God my Savior, for he has been mindful of the humble state of his servant. From now on all generations will call me blessed, for the Mighty One has done great things for me—holy is his name. His mercy extends to those who fear him, from generation to generation. He has performed mighty deeds with his arm; he has scattered those who are proud in their inmost thoughts. He has brought down rulers from their thrones but has lifted up the humble. He has filled the hungry with good things but has sent the rich away empty. He has helped his servant Israel, remembering to be merciful to Abraham and his descendants for ever, just as he promised our ancestors.[4]

In the aftermath of her dramatic encounter with the angel, Mary re-writes the story of her life, placing her story within the larger narrative of Abraham. She now sees her life as being filled with significance and honor, a life that has been radically interrupted by the beautiful, transforming, graceful initiative of God. For each of us the invitation to narrate the stories that we inhabit in new, imaginative, and faith-filled ways is ever present.

4. Luke 1:46–55.

4

Language

IN OUR PURSUIT TO understand the dynamics of transformation we have now arrived at the role of language. It is a self evident observation to state that our lives are lived linguistically. We live amidst shared tales, instructions, euphemisms, metaphors, enouragements, put-downs, jokes, hints, gossip, insinuations, commands . . . the list of linguistic interventions is seemingly endless. All of these have the power to bring us into a spacious place of growth or to do just the opposite, to close down, to condemn, and to curse. At its very best poetic metaphorical language, which is often the language of Scripture, acts upon us as a conduit for the grace of God. Kevin Vanhoozer puts it like this:

> The poetic word functions sacramentally. The sacramental function of the poetic and religious text consists above all in its power to disclose a graced world over and above the natural world.[1]

Our guide into the world of language in this chapter will be Ludwig Wittgenstein. Ludwig Wittgenstein may seem an unlikely choice of guide into the mysteries of human transformation. He was a mid-twentieth century Austrian philosopher and school teacher who became a Cambridge professor that many would claim changed the course of philosophy. Wittgenstein was an enigmatic figure who is impossible to categorize. He was neither an

---

1 Vanhoozer, *Biblical Narrative*, 170.

atheist nor a person of faith, although he was shaped by a Christian upbringing and was driven by a passion to philosophize about the nature of philosophy itself. Wittgenstein claimed that many of the most knotted philosophical conundrums originated in a failure to appreciate how language works. The meaning of language, he insisted, is found not in dictionary definitions, but rather in the way in which language is used in ordinary speech. Language finds itself situated in the "games" that we all use when we converse. Every language is both the product of a culture from which it emerges and also the shaper of that culture. Language oscillates backwards and forwards between the act of articulation pouring forth from within a culture and its return to that same culture in new and innovative ways.

Compare for example ancient Hebrew, the language of the Old Testament, and contemporary German. Hebrew sentences tend to begin with a verb, a statement of action and intent. This makes Hebrew sound very vibrant and dynamic, emerging from a culture that placed a high value on the way that daily life was actually lived. Movement, choice, doing, performing, listening, tending, harvesting, obeying, worshipping, cultivating—these are the stuff of life in the ancient world of the Hebrews. It may come as no surprise therefore to find that many Hebrew nouns are derived from verbs. One example is the word *yetser*, meaning "to form." It is the word used in the Genesis creation story describing the actions of Yahweh. Yahweh is the divine artist who imagines, shapes, sculpts, and brings into being. Listen to the words of Genesis 2:7.

> [T]hen the Lord God formed (*yester*) the man of dust from the ground and breathed into his nostrils the breath of life, and the man became a living creature.

The same linguistic root is used in Jeremiah 18:1–4.

> The word that came to Jeremiah from the LORD: "Arise, and go down to the potter's house, and there I will let you hear my words." So I went down to the potter's house, and there he was working at his wheel. And the vessel he was making of clay was spoiled in the potter's hand, and

he reworked it into another vessel, as it seemed good to
the potter to do.

Here the word translated as *potter* literally means "the one who
shapes." It is a derivative of the verb *yetser* and as a noun it is written
yetsar. The noun becomes the concrete form of the verb. One senses that the Hebrew culture prioritized the performing of an action,
for the essence of life was rooted in the ordinary everyday choices
that one makes. By contrast, German sentences, especially those
long sentences with subordinate clauses, tend to push the verbs to
the very end of the sentence. One has to wait until the end of the
sentence to be sure of the kind of action that is being performed.
Clearly it is impossible to generalize about entire languages, but
it is surely instructive to observe how different languages possess
very diverse language rules, playing very different language games,
and thus shaping the way in which a cultural mindset is formed.

Language rules don't simply differ at the level of whole languages, such as Hebrew and German, but each language also find
itself used in many diverse social situations (e.g., giving a political speech, delivering a mathematics lecture, telling jokes, buying
fruit, playing sport, praying to God) that, according to Wittgenstein, are all governed by their own set of rules for word use.

Wittgenstein was consumed with exploring how such language
games functioned and how this might impact philosophical questions of meaning. Consider this excerpt from his book *Philosophical
Investigations* in which he explores the meaning of the word "king."

> When one shews someone the king in chess and says:
> "This is the king," this does not tell him the use of this
> piece—unless he already knows the rules of the game up
> to this last point: the shape of the king. You could imagine
> his having learnt the rules of the game without ever hav-
> ing been shewn an actual piece. The shape of the chess-
> man corresponds here to the sound or shape of a word.
> One can also imagine someone's having learnt the game
> without ever learning or formulating rules. He might
> have learnt quite simple board games first, by watching,
> and have progressed to more and more complicated ones.
> He too might be given the explanation "This is the king."

If, for instance, he were being shewn chessmen of a shape he was not used to. This explanation again only tells him the use of the piece because, as we might say, the place for it was already prepared. Or even: we shall only say that it tells him the use, if the place is already prepared. And in this case it is so, not because the person to whom we give the explanation already knows rules, but because in another sense he is already master of a game. Consider this further case: I am explaining chess to someone; and I begin by pointing to a chessman and saying: "This is the king; it can move like this . . . and so on."—In this case we shall say: the words "This is the king" (or "This is called the 'king'") are a definition only if the learner already "knows what a piece in a game is." That is, if he has already played other games, or has watched other people playing "and understood"—and similar things. Further, only under these conditions will he be able to ask relevantly in the course of learning the game: "What do you call this?"—that is, this piece in a game.[2]

The context of these thoughts lie in an imaginary conversation between chess players. In this scenario to utter the word "king" could be simply a way of referring to a chess piece or perhaps to its particular shape. Alternatively, to say "this is a king" could mean far more than a referential description of a piece on the board but, by implication, a description of its function within the game. To appreciate the latter meaning is to presuppose that one understands the whole principle of playing games on a board in which there are precise rules that must be adhered to. Wittgenstein is here claiming that language usage is more than something that is simply ostensive.

Ostensive ideas about the acquisition of language are grounded upon the assumption that language works by making a connection between a sound and an object. Wittgenstein uses a passage from Augustine's *Confessions* with which to engage and the following extensive quotation from Augustine's biographical writing illustrates the ostensive theory of language.

2. Wittgenstein, *Philosophical Investigations,* Aphorisms 31–38.

I not, then, as I grew out of infancy, come next to boy-
hood, or rather did it not come to me and succeed my
infancy? My infancy did not go away (for where would
it go?) It was simply no longer present; and I was no longer an infant who could not speak, but now a chattering
boy. I remember this, and I have since observed how I
learned to speak. My elders did not teach me words by
rote, as they taught me my letters afterward. But I myself,
when I was unable to communicate all I wished to say
to whomever I wished by means of whimperings and
grunts and various gestures of my limbs (which I used
to reinforce my demands), I myself repeated the sounds
already stored in my memory by the mind which thou,
O my God, hadst given me. When they called some thing
by name and pointed it out while they spoke, I saw it and
realized that the thing they wished to indicate was called
by the name they then uttered. And what they meant was
made plain by the gestures of their bodies, by a kind of
natural language, common to all nations, which express-
es itself through changes of countenance, glances of the
eye, gestures and intonations which indicate a disposi-
tion and attitude—either to seek or to possess, to reject
or to avoid. So it was that by frequently hearing words, in
different phrases, I gradually identified the objects which
the words stood for and, having formed my mouth to
repeat these signs, I was thereby able to express my will.
Thus I exchanged with those about me the verbal signs
by which we express our wishes and advanced deeper
into the stormy fellowship of human life, depending all
the while upon the authority of my parents and the be-
hest of my elders.[3]

In his later work, *The Philosophical Investigations*, Wittgenstein found himself refuting this notion of Augustine. Merely to
point to an object and to give it a name—which is how all of us
began to learn our mother tongue—is part of the story. Language
only carries meaning in the context that it is used, which suggests
that language is far more slippery, dynamic, and supple than simple
dictionary definitions. One example from a local Northern Irish

3. Augustine, *Confessions*, 1.8.

dialect illustrates this. If one utters the phrase: "he'd be a friend of mine" in County Tyrone, it is not a conditional statement (he would be a friend of mine *if . . .*) nor does it mean that the person is a "friend" in the more conventional use of the term. It means quite simply that the person being identified is a close relative. "He'd be a far out friend of mine" therefore means that the person in question is a distant relation. Speaking a language, claims Wittgenstein, is part of a form of life and, as is self-evident, forms of life are many and varied. "How should we get into conflict with the truth," writes Wittgenstein, "if our footrules were made of very soft rubber, instead of wood and steel?"[4]

If the meaning of language can alter according to usage then it contains a power that is potentially transformative. A few biblical examples may illustrate the subversive nature of language and the way in which poetic forms of speech can call transformation forth. During the trial of Christ recorded for us in John 18 this conversation, also revolving around the word "king," is recounted.

> Then Pilate went back inside the palace. He called for Jesus and asked him, "Are you the king of the Jews?" Jesus said, "Is that your own question, or did other people tell you about me?" Pilate said, "I'm not a Jew! It was your own people and their leading priests who brought you before me. What have you done wrong?" Jesus said, "My kingdom does not belong to this world. If it did, my servants would fight so that I would not be handed over to the Jewish leaders. No, my kingdom is not an earthly one." Pilate said, "So you are a king." Jesus answered, "You are right to say that I am a king. I was born for this: to tell people about the truth. That is why I came into the world. And everyone who belongs to the truth listens to me." Pilate said, "What is truth?"

The key question here concerned the meaning of the word "king," as there are three possible understandings of the word. Firstly, it is evident that Pilate had a very clear idea as to the meaning of this word. For him, a king was a political position that authorized

---

4. Wittgenstein, *Remarks on the Foundations of Mathematics*, 5.

the use of power over subjects within a kingdom. Pilate's position as the fifth prefect of the province of Judea during the Roman occupation of the land conferred on him significant responsibility, together with the power to rule. He was in effect a "king." Yet into his province arises a popular leader, teacher, and healer who is acclaimed by the people to also be a "king." In the minds of the Jewish people this kingship was confined to them alone and not to the Gentile inhabitants of the land. His kingship fulfilled for them the hopes and longings of an oppressed people in an occupied land. This is the second understanding of the word "king." Thirdly, Jesus himself offers an entirely different perspective. "My kingdom does not belong to this world," he claims. He uses the same term as both Pilate and the Jewish people, but uses the word in a novel way. His kingship is of a more mysterious nature, not defined geographically, not limited to one nation or people group, and displaying non-violent characteristics. His use of the word "king" did not correspond to any known category. One could only understand what Jesus meant by the word "king" by observing and describing how such a king behaved. This is what Wittgenstein meant by the grammar of the word "king." It is how it is *used* that determines its meaning, and not its assumed connotation.

It must have been a thoroughly confusing conversation for Pilate. An ordinary, common word was being used with a definition that was, supposedly, uniformly agreed upon. Christ subverts that definition by claiming that the only way in which his use of the word "king" can be understood is by observing how the subjects of such a king function in society. Such subjects do not take up arms, they do not try to protect this king from harm, they do not behave in the normal expected way of people who belong to a kingdom. If this is a kingdom that does not function in the way that other kingdoms do then this sheds light on the kind of king Jesus claims to be. This is precisely the kind of language game to which Ludwig Wittgenstein drew attention. Jesus was indeed toying with Pilate, using language playfully, metaphorically, subversively. The American liturgist Gail Ramshaw[5] states quite simply

5. Ramshaw, *Liturgical Language*.

that Christianity requires metaphoric thinking. Metaphor is the kind of slippery language that resists constraint and that refuses to have its meaning exhausted. It always allows for, even demands, an "overflow of possibilities," to borrow a phrase from the French philosopher Paul Ricoeur.

The answer that Jesus gave illuminates the way in which much biblical language works. His answer was both disruptive and evocative. It was disruptive in that his use of the word "king" subverted the accepted rules of the language game surrounding the word. If the accepted language rules of the word king referred to a visible, definable, domain of control then for Jesus to accept this appellation was a disruptive act. He willingly took the name upon himself yet rejected the normal language game associated with that one word. In doing so he was acting as a true prophet. The task of the biblical prophet is to subvert and disrupt the comfortable, known world, where words have agreed meanings and accepted usage. The prophet points to another possible world, a world yet to come into existence. Hear the confusing, disturbing words of the prophet Isaiah:

> The wolf shall dwell with the lamb,
>   and the leopard shall lie down with the young goat,
> and the calf and the lion and the fattened calf together;
>   and a little child shall lead them.
> The cow and the bear shall graze;
>   their young shall lie down together;
>   and the lion shall eat straw like the ox.
> The nursing child shall play over the hole of the cobra,
>   and the weaned child shall put his hand on the adder's
>   den.[6]

Isaiah disrupts the way in which language is expected to work. To say "this is a leopard" is not only to make an ostensive statement—"look over there, a leopard!"—but to hint also at the carnivorous behavior of the animal. Yet Isaiah claims that this predator will, one day, lie down peacefully with its prey. There will be no devouring and tearing, but simply contentment. Prophetic

---

6. Isa 11:6–8.

speech deconstructs language games, disrupts expectations, disorientates, confuses. Such speech is profoundly necessary if any signs of transformation are to occur.

Within this exploration of the transformative power of language it is instructive to observe how Ignatius of Loyola used the language of "king" in one of his spiritual exercises. The Ignatian Spiritual Exercises were written in the early sixteenth century in order to provide a means of bringing about deep transformation in the lives of those who chose to use them. One of the exercises is known as "The call of the king." Ignatius writes:

> First, I will place before my mind a human king, chosen by God our Lord himself, whom all Christian princes and all Christian persons reverence and obey. Second, I will observe how this king speaks to all his people, saying, "My will is to conquer the whole land of the infidels. Hence, whoever wishes to come with me has to be content with the same food I eat, and the drink, and the clothing which I wear, and so forth. So too each one must labor with me during the day, and keep watch in the night, and so on, so that later each may have a part with me in the victory, just as each has shared in the toil." Third, I will consider what good subjects ought to respond to a king so generous and kind; and how, consequently, if someone did not answer his call, he would be scorned and upbraided by everyone and accounted as an unworthy knight.[7]

This imaginative exercise, couched in the language and thought forms of sixteenth-century Spain, invites the person engaging in the spiritual reflection to hear the call of an earthly king. "How would you respond" writes Ignatius, "if an earthly king summons you to engage in loyal acts of heroism, to courageously leave the comforts of home and go wherever such a ruler may send you? Would that not be the greatest honor and would a refusal of such a call bring down disgrace and shame upon your head?" Such exercises were intended to allow the one using them to feel the affective response in one's soul to such a call. The Call of the King exercise

7. Ignatius, *Spiritual Exercises and Selected Works*, 146.

often elicited a greater sense of faith-filled fearlessness on the part of those who completed the meditation. Ignatius then invites the participant to transfer that same experience on to the call of King Jesus, noticing if there are any similarities or differences in the way in which a response emerges.

> If we give consideration to such a call from the temporal king to his subjects, how much more worthy of our consideration it is to gaze upon Christ our Lord, the eternal King, and all the world assembled before him. He calls to them all, and to each person in particular he says: "My will is to conquer the whole world and all my enemies, and thus to enter into the glory of my Father. Therefore, whoever wishes to come with me must labor with me, so that through following me in the pain he or she may follow me also in the glory."[8]

This exercise clearly flows out of his own experience. Born in 1491 in the Basque town of Azpetitia, Ignatius came from a noble family. In his early life he worked as the pageboy of the royal treasurer and accompanied his master to the royal court. He later became a soldier and was involved in the siege of Pamplona by the French in 1521. It was here that his life changed dramatically when he was injured by a cannonball in his leg. The fracture was set and reset, resulting in a convalescence that lasted nearly ten months. During this period his encounters with God were particularly formative. He noticed that when he dreamt of doing heroic deeds on the battlefield the experience left him feeling drained and exhausted. By contrast, when he imagined himself performing great adventures for the sake of Christ he felt invigorated and refreshed. It was by paying attention to the movements within his soul that he was persuaded to completely alter the course of his career. His dissatisfaction with the way he had been living was highlighted by the allure of following Christ; it was as if he was being divinely courted. This attentiveness to God's actions within him became a key feature of his spiritual development. From that time onwards he vowed that he would be a soldier for Christ. He exchanged his

8. Ibid., 147.

clothes for those of a poor man, he went on a pilgrimage to Jerusalem, he studied avidly, both in Paris and in Rome, and had a number of significant spiritual experiences that shaped his values and changed the course of his life. One of these occurred at Manresa in 1522, where he remained for several months. During this time he had a visionary experience in a cave on the banks of the river Cardoner. Karl Rahner claims that from that point onwards

> [h]e saw Jesus as the gentle King and lord who came to fulfill the spread of the kingdom of God which had dawned. Ignatius sensed his vocation to become a worker with and for Christ.[9]

The new transformative language of "king" was one of the keys that unlocked the door to an entirely new way of life for Ignatius.

In addition to this evocative pull of language, the converse is equally true, for certain forms of speech can also possess a blocking, impeding power. The well known story of the journey towards Canaan illustrates this. In Numbers 13 we read of the initial exploration of the promised land by a group of spies. Upon their return the men gave a report to the community about their exploits. One group described the land as flowing with milk and honey, waiting to be enjoyed; another group reported that it was a land of great danger, inhabited by huge giants. The desert community were then faced with the challenge of responding to the phrase "promised land." What did this phrase mean? What did it signify? To what did it refer? Ostensively it simply referred to a piece of land west of the River Jordan. Yet its meaning was clearly far more significant than that. In the minds of a tiny minority of those who heard the phrase it was profoundly evocative. It allured, pulled towards, empowered, and ennobled. Yet for the majority it was repellent and dangerous. "That night all the people of the community raised their voices and wept aloud" (Num 14:1). The same words were used, the same phrasing referring to the same place, yet these words were understood and received in entirely different ways. For

---

9. Rahner, *Ignatius of Loyola*, 49.

the majority of the Israelites in the desert, "promised land" was a place to be avoided.

So what has this discussion about language games to do with human transformation today? Everything. We inhabit a world that is founded linguistically. Human experience is communicated and interpreted through language, which lends it the power to both destroy and to renew.

The simple call of Christ to *come follow me* is not as simple as it might first appear. The words are inevitably filtered through the linguistic paradigms of our own experience of life. And it is precisely during that filtering process that meanings and interpretations are formed and accepted as the truth. The legacy of Wittgenstein is that "truth" usually has rubber feet rather than steel soles. This is not to say that Wittgenstein embraced skepticism as a life position. Nothing could be further from the truth. He merely demonstrated how language is rooted in the cultural life of a community and genuine meaning is located there too. Language is the handmaiden of anthropology, which in turn is the medium through which the Word of the Lord is mediated to us. So the imperative to *come follow me* raises big questions about who is the "me" that we are to called to "follow" and who is the "me" that hears that invitation. Does the word "follow" mean what I think it might mean? A whole host of questions have to be negotiated, re-imagined, and re-interpreted before any committed response can be offered. This is the challenge of transformation, to hear the language of Scripture as the voice of God made profoundly personal.

This chapter concludes with an excerpt of a transcript that formed part of a conversation with Alison. Alison grew up in a Christian home characterized by an evangelical pietism. During her childhood and adolescence there was much talk in the home about the need for a radical obedience to Christ combined with an insistence on the necessity of regular confession of sin. There was a strong emphasis on God being understood as Mighty, Holy, and Sovereign. Since leaving the family home some ten years ago she had been able to identify significant ways in which she is currently undergoing transformation. This transformation could be seen in her new understanding of who she is and a fresh way in which she understands the nature of God. She was asked the question, "Looking back over the past ten years, how has your perception of the nature of God changed?" What she says is highly instructive.

> What has started to happen is a loosening up of the categories of "inside" and "outside," like me being the subject and then there is God as the object. I don't relate to the words of my childhood any longer—words like Mighty and Holy. I am now thinking more of God and me as one. I don't relate to the word "Savior" any more. God for me is more of a friend or a companion . . . someone who is always there for me. I feel more secure in my faith now, I don't have to try so hard.

In this short extract Alison mentions that words depicting God that had been used during her upbringing no longer contained any positive resonance and had gradually begun to function as braking mechanism for her. They did not invite or attract, but rather the opposite, they repelled her and she noticed that they closed her heart and soul down. Holy, Mighty, and Savior as names for God only served to emphasize for her the feeling of difference, distance, hierarchy, and an imbalance of power. They reinforced the sense of the subject–object gulf and did nothing whatsoever to engender intimacy. This suggests that the way in which these words had been used in a language game in her experience had had a negative effect. Even if one were to offer an explanation as to how these words are deployed within biblical linguistic contexts one suspects that the emotional memory of their usage in her own life would have been a more powerful influence on their reception. Over the years she had begun to search for alternative words for God that attracted her. Such words were companion, friend, someone who is there for me, being one with God. These appellations contained a much greater sense of transformative magnetism. The new set of descriptors were ones that bridged an apparent divide that she had perceived between her as the subject and God as the object of the relationship. The words were not so much ways of defining the character of God but rather, ways of depicting the more intimate nature of the relationship that she now felt that she had with God. This new relational space offered her a deeper sense of security, a place of acceptance, somewhere that did not require the constant effort of having to try harder. It may be that in the future she will sense the need to revisit those older names for God and find a new, perhaps deeper resonances there. The process of transformation is one of constantly re-negotiating the same issues time and again from different vantage points and with potentially very different outcomes.

The depictions of God that Alison finds most problematic—Holy, Mighty, Savior—are words that belong to a metaphysical sphere. For her they sound as if they are detached from the real world of our ordinary everyday existence, the world of cars, trees, cows, and supermarkets. They depict a hidden realm from which our lived experience is detached by a great gulf. The words that describe God that Alison found to be most endearing—companion, friend, someone who is there for me—are of a quite different order. They emerge from the rough ground of ordinary life where there is sufficient "friction" for them to contain significance. Wittgenstein claimed that it is precisely here in this real world of joy and pain, fulfillment and frustration, suffering and pleasure that language is located and has meaning. It is here that language about God is found too. For some people the language of God's might, power, sovereignty, and holiness depicts a hidden, ethereal world, a place that is too slippery for there to be sufficient friction for language to carry any authentic meaning. Alison's move towards a more earthed, transforming spirituality is analogous to the way in which Wittgenstein claimed language was always rooted within a lived life.

5

Culture

IN WHAT WAY DOES transforming faith find expression within the cultures that we inhabit? This is a delicate and entangled issue to negotiate. All of us have emerged into adulthood having been shaped by the language, the customs, the food, the traditions, and the physical environment of our childhood and adolescence. We are bound to these cultural norms by deep emotional roots. To step back and assess our own culture dispassionately is an exercise in mental and spiritual gymnastics. It is usually only when we move away from our own cultural moorings and enter an entirely different culture that we can, from a distance, develop some alternative insights. It is an exercise in discerning how faith engages with the myriad different ways in which human societies organize themselves. This chapter will explore this question in the company of one major thinker in the area of faith and culture—the theologian and ethicist, H. Richard Niebuhr. Niebuhr was an American theologian who explored the borderland where Christian expression and culture touch each other. Niebuhr was born in Missouri and became one of the most significant Christian ethicists of the twentieth century. His most influential book, *Christ and Culture*, explored the history of the Christian church's engagement with culture over the centuries. Although subsequent generations of theologians have taken issue with the way in which Niebuhr presents his ideas, his book remains a good basis from which our engagement with this issue can begin. In this book he divides the varying responses into five broad categories or types. A brief outline of them is listed here.

CHRIST AGAINST CULTURE

This position depicts two separate worlds. There is the world of Christian allegiance that calls Christ's disciples to seek to establish a separate community characterized by the values of the kingdom of heaven. This stands in stark contrast to the world that we know and already inhabit, a place of very different values and aspirations. There can be no substantial dialogue between these two spheres due to the claims of Christian discipleship to be separate, untainted by the claims of loyalty to any other culture. This split between the so called material and spiritual realms implies that there is a rejection of human cultures. In this view, Christ transcends all human cultures and judges them to be deficient. In the early centuries of the Christian church such notions of separatism were first put forward in the works of some of the best known early Christian documents; books such as *The Teaching of the Twelve*, *The Shepherd of Hermas*, *The Epistle of Barnabas* and *The First Epistle of Clement*. The essence of these publications was to assert that Christ chose to create a peculiar people who lived separated lives. One may also cite the world of the Amish or the Hutterites in various parts of the United States, communities that have sought over the centuries to preserve their own separate distinct Christian culture in the face of a continually changing, diverse, and dynamic American society. Some brands of contemporary evangelical fundamentalism might also espouse views that are closely allied to this category that Niebuhr puts forward.

THE CHRIST OF CULTURE

At the other end of the spectrum, claims Niebuhr, there is the position which he labels The Christ of Culture. According to this view the tension between the church and the world is far less marked.

Culture is interpreted through Christ in such a way that some, although not all, aspects of culture are already imbued with the presence and validation of Christ. "All along the line," states Niebuhr, "the tendency in the movement is to identify Jesus with the immanent divine spirit that works in men." It is a position that tends to favor Christ as a mystical figure and in the early days of the church groups known as gnostics emerged who, Niebuhr claims, epitomize this position. This is how Niebuhr depicts the gnostics' position with reference to engaging with culture.

> A Gnostic had no reason for refusing to pay homage to Caesar or to participate in war; though perhaps he had no compelling reason, apart from social pressure, for yielding to the mores and the laws. If he was too enlightened to take seriously the popular and official worship of idols, he was also too enlightened to make an issue out of its rejection; and martyrdom he scorned.[1]

These first two positions represent two ends of a continuum, from outright rejection of culture at one end to accommodation at the other. In between these two poles lie other more graduated responses.

CHRIST ABOVE CULTURE

This view does not set Christ against culture in hostility but seeks a synthesis of the two kingdoms. There may be elements of culture that are worthy, reflecting something of the presence of Christ and which the grace of God can, over time, perfect. As Niebuhr expressed it, those who take the view that Christ is above culture

> cannot separate the works of human culture from the grace of God, for all those works are possible only by grace. But neither can they separate the experience of grace from cultural activity; for how can men love the

---

1. Niebuhr, *Christ and Culture*, 87.

unseen God in response to His love without serving the
visible brother in human society?[2]

In Christian history it is Thomas Aquinas, the thirteenth-
century Dominican friar, who gave greatest impetus to this view.
Aquinas did not see Christ and culture as being in eternal opposition to each other. His approach was a both-and one, albeit with
Christ remaining high above culture and not uncritically identified with it. Aquinas was a great synthesist, seeking to combine
"state and church, civic and Christian values, natural and divine
laws, Christ and culture."[3] It was through the influence of Aquinas
that the great academic institutions of Europe gained their impetus, with the church supporting and endorsing the role of the state
whenever there was deemed to be shared values.

CHRIST AND CULTURE IN PARADOX

This designation coined by Niebuhr describes what he sees as a
dualist position. The paradox is that both the culture of Christ and
the culture of this world can and do coexist, inevitably, side-by-
side. It is also a both-and solution to the question of how faith is
expressed culturally. He cites the most well known exponent of this
view—Martin Luther. In Luther's two works, *Treatise on Christian
Liberty* and *Against the Robbing and Murdering Hordes of Peasants*,
Luther sets forth two apparently contradictory and paradoxical
views. In *Christian Liberty*, Luther urges his readers that

> from faith flows forth love and joy in the Lord, and from
> love a joyful, willing, and free mind that serves one's
> neighbor willingly and takes no account of gratitude or
> ingratitude, of praise or blame, of gain or loss.[4]

Yet in his pamphlet written about the *Hordes of Peasants*, he states
that

2. Ibid., 119.
3. Ibid., 130.
4. Ibid., 170.

a prince or Lord must remember in this case that he is God's minister and the servant of his wrath to whom the sword is committed for use upon such fellows. . . . Here there is no time for sleeping; no place for patience or mercy. It is the time of the sword, not the day of grace.[5]

It is as if Luther claims that there are two modes of being, one private, one public, and these two operate according to very different modes of conduct. Both, claims Luther, are distinct ways of offering service to God, although they would appear to be in paradoxical conflict with one another.

CHRIST THE TRANSFORMER OF CULTURE

In this, the fifth and final classification, Niebuhr sets out what is generally regarded to be his favored position. Niebuhr depicts the view that culture provides the raw material with which Christians can shape society towards a Christian vision. Culture is given to the church in order that it might be transformed. The biblical metaphors of salt, yeast, and light are particularly pertinent here, highlighting the potential for culture to be quietly infiltrated with the gospel, which spreads pervasively until society is itself transformed.

This classification that Niebuhr offers illustrates how, over the centuries, the church has attempted to address the question of developing a relationship with the prevailing culture. Should it be condoned, confronted, or withdrawn from? In doing so Niebuhr illustrates how each particular cultural stance is the outworking of three key theological issues.

The first of these is a theology of creation. Human cultures are unavoidably rooted in the created world. If one sees creation as a distraction from the supposedly more important and higher business of spiritual growth then it follows that one might develop a dismissive attitude to it. Creation becomes merely the stage upon which the main event, namely private interior spirituality,

5. Ibid., 170.

is performed. Or, by contrast, one might view creation as something to be tamed and subdued, to be brought under the rule and domination of human agency. Or, further still, creation could be seen as the great adversary from which the Christian church must of necessity withdraw for the sake of purity and radical obedience. The way in which creation is viewed necessarily determines the shape and texture of cultural engagement.

The second issue concerns Trinitarian theology. Trinitarian theology asserts that the world that we inhabit is founded on an understanding of God who is revealed as being both intrinsically relational and incarnational. When God is known as the Father, the Son, and the Spirit who are in eternal communion with each other then a high value is placed upon relational engagement rather than withdrawal. If God is relational then we too, who are made in his image, are created to be relational. If the Son is the one who became flesh, dwelt amongst us, chopped wood, told stories, met the outcast, and got his hands dirty, then we too have the same impetus to be thoroughly "incarnated" in our surrounding culture. Christ's footprints on the soil of Galilee display an earthy engagement with the culture of his day.

The third theological issue concerns the dimension, the position, and the influence of the "kingdom of heaven," however one defines what this term means. When Christ announced that this kingdom had already broken into our world and would one day be fully completed, he depicted an unseen yet profoundly real alternative cultural reality. This eschatological kingdom was radically different to any kingdom that was known. Its cultural rules, its traditions, its geography, and its concept of time could not be categorized in any known way or by reference to any known criteria. This kingdom coexists alongside every other human cultural convention, waiting, lurking even, for moments of exposure. The simultaneous presence of two kingdoms, side-by-side, overlapping perhaps, competing with one another is the stuff that the Christ and culture debate is made of.

On a personal level I have always found the relationship between faith in Christ and culture both endlessly fascinating and fraught with difficulty. My journey through life has afforded me the opportunities to live in some very disparate cultures—from my birthplace in South Africa, to a childhood in the suburbs of London, to Germany, Nigeria, and rural Northern Ireland. Living in a culture that has not been my own has always thrown into very sharp focus the differences that exist between societies. Each one has developed traditions and cultural practices that have demanded my full attention and respect. Some examples from my own experience may illustrate this.

In Germany the cultural values of efficiency and self-sufficiency are prized. Children are expected to learn the skills of self-determination from a young age and to do so with an attention to detail that is often very impressive. Whereas in England young children are often taxied to school, in Germany it is more common to see young children walking or cycling significant distances. In Northern Ireland by way of contrast, the enjoyment of "craic" is a vital part of the culture. Craic, meaning conversation, storytelling, and laughter is the essential quality that makes society tick. It is not uncommon to hear of the assessment of another person according to the amount of craic that is evident. One may be highly proficient at many tasks, thoroughly reliable, creative, and interesting, but if there is no craic something is sorely amiss.

In the early 1980s my wife and I travelled to Nigeria in order to take up teaching posts in a school located in a remote rural district in the centre of the country. A large part of the motivation for making such a risky move was to examine which parts of my faith were culturally determined and which were transferable across cultures. I discovered that extensive greeting rituals were absolutely essential for social functioning, gender roles were often highly specific, and hospitality was highly valued. The uninvited stranger at the door was always welcomed and invited into the home to share a family meal. Yet family meals may also have seen a segregation of the sexes, with the men and boys in one room and the women and girls eating outside in the backyard what the men had left. After three years I left the country with more questions than answers concerning the relationship between faith and culture.

One small example may illustrate my dilemma. The nearby church had been built many years earlier by missionaries from Northern Ireland and they had named it "The Ulster Church." On Sundays the congregation of approximately 1,000 Nigerian worshippers sang with gusto from the hymn book that the missionaries had brought with them. I will never forget my puzzlement when one of their favorite songs, "All things bright and beautiful" was sung, including the line referring to the "purple headed mountain." The hymn writer, Cecil Frances Alexander, had written this hymn in the late nineteenth century while living in the market town of Strabane, County Tyrone. No doubt the hills of her native Ireland were in mind when she penned these verses. Sung in the sweltering tropical heat at the height of the dusty African dry season it felt rather incongruous.

Culture is the cradle that holds our existence and determines the boundaries, the expectations, the permissions, as well as the prohibitions of those who dwell within its borders. This is immediately problematic in any attempt to express the Christian faith. The manifestation of the good news of the gospel in culture is concerned with the ushering in of an entirely new dimension to society, a dimension that possesses something of the fragrance of the kingdom of heaven that Jesus so boldly declared had arrived. If we are in the process of being transformed into the likeness of Christ the challenge is to discern what this looks like within the local culture where we are placed. This was graphically brought home to me recently when a colleague described an occasion when he travelled to Finland for conference with other clergy. Half way through proceedings all the delegates retired to the nearby sauna—segregated according to gender—where all the men sat together completely naked discussing the next item on the agenda. Such an activity would be unthinkable in Britain or the USA.

So in what way does the Christian faith engage with such a range of different cultures? Can the good news of Jesus Christ metamorphose, chameleon like, altering its texture and hue according to its cultural backdrop? In order to address that question it may be useful to notice the component elements that are found in any culture across the globe. Each culture possesses four anchorage points that hold it in place and offer the means of maintaining social cohesion for a particular group. These anchorage points are:

- *An agreed collection of shared practices.* Practices come in a million different ways, from particular rituals that are performed at certain times of the year, modes of dress, types of dancing performed, or the preparation of certain foods.

- *A set of values.* Values undergird these practices and determine the manner in which they are performed and the degree of priority allocated to each one.

- *A range of philosophical or theological convictions.* These too may manifest themselves in a huge range of possibilities concerning, for example, the way in which the universe is ordered, the character of God (if indeed there is a god), and the particular capabilities and responsibilities of humanity.

- *A deep connection with history.* Cultural practices seek to build a sense of continuity between the past and the present.

These four combine to construct a culture that is usually limited in its scope by ethnicity or geography or by both of these. An example from Northern Ireland may illustrate how these points of reference hold a culture securely in place. The Orange Order is a Protestant society that was formed to preserve the memory of the role of King William of Orange in 1690 at the Battle of the Boyne. King William, a Dutchman, defeated the English Roman Catholic King James II at the River Boyne, thus preserving the Reformed heritage in parts of Ireland and thereby preventing a Catholic king from establishing a foothold. The four anchorage points outlined above can be clearly seen within this cultural phenomenon.

- *Practices:* The practices of the present day Orange Order thus involve the wearing of a uniform (an orange sash to symbolize the link with the Netherlands), marching through the streets during the months of July and August, the flying of flags, and the construction of memorials to the events of the late seventeenth century.

- *Values:* It values godly living, strenuous opposition to Roman Catholicism, and the defense of the Reformed Christian faith.[6]

- *Convictions:* The Orange Order holds to the conviction that the "Protestant Religion" is correct and Roman Catholic theology is intrinsically false. The strongest political conviction of the Order concerns the preservation of a union with the United Kingdom.

- *History:* Through the use of historical symbols on banners, flags, and emblems, a strong link with the past is maintained.

For many people in Northern Ireland the Orange Order is a vital, living, and essential part of their culture. The cultural practices, the undergirding values, the convictions, and the connection with

---

6. QUALIFICATIONS OF AN ORANGEMAN

An Orangeman should have a sincere love and veneration for his Heavenly Father; a humble and steadfast faith in Jesus Christ, the Saviour of mankind, believing in Him as the only Mediator between God and man. He should cultivate truth and justice, brotherly kindness and charity, devotion and piety, concord and unity, and obedience to the laws; his deportment should be gentle and compassionate, kind and courteous; he should seek the society of the virtuous, and avoid that of the evil; he should honour and diligently study the Holy Scriptures, and make them the rule of his faith and practice; he should love, uphold, and defend the Protestant religion, and sincerely desire and endeavour to propagate its doctrines and precepts; he should strenuously oppose the fatal errors and doctrines of the Church of Rome, and scrupulously avoid countenancing (by his presence or otherwise) any act or ceremony of Popish Worship; he should, by all lawful means, resist the ascendancy of that Church, its encroachments, and the extension of its power, ever abstaining from all uncharitable words, actions, or sentiments towards his Roman Catholic brethren; he should remember to keep holy the Sabbath day, and attend the public worship of God, and diligently train up his offspring, and all under his control, in the fear of God, and in the Protestant faith; he should never take the name of God in vain, but abstain from all cursing and profane language, and use every opportunity of discouraging those, and all other sinful practices, in others; his conduct should be guided by wisdom and prudence, and marked by honesty, temperance, and sobriety; the glory of God and the welfare of man, the honour of his Sovereign, and the good of his country, should be the motives of his actions. (http://www.citygrandlodge.com/qualifications.html)

history are intertwined in such a way as to ensure that the Orange Order is perpetuated in each succeeding generation.

In negotiating our relationship with culture it may be useful to assess how transforming faith engages with the four points outlined above. To an outsider it is the practices that are initially most evident, and participation in the practices is usually the entrance into cultural understanding and acceptance. Some practices are ethically neutral and intrinsically essential for society to function well. Take, for example, the significance of the left hand in Nigerian culture. The right hand is the hand to be used for performing greetings or in giving and receiving. The left hand is never to be used for such purposes and to do so is deemed to be highly insulting. Respecting and honoring this aspect of Nigerian culture is a necessity if one is to live in peace and harmony. Each society has its own set of such practices with which Christian faith needs to have no argument. To respect these practices is the outworking of incarnational presence and it demands a level of submission to this limitation.

Not all practices, however, are ethically neutral. It is when they express an underlying set of values that are at odds with the coming kingdom of Christ that subversive action is demanded. The early Christian church was immediately faced with the question of negotiating the interface between their faith in Christ and the culture in which they lived. Roman society, like ours, was imbued with its own norms and cultural expectations. It was expected, for example, that as you entered a typical Roman home deference was shown to a statue of a Roman god placed strategically in the house. This was standard accepted practice. As soon as the early Christians refused to conform to this practice, insisting that their new found faith in Christ would not permit them to participate in this standard practice, then it was not long before they were shunned and excluded from society. The letter to the Hebrews is addressed to precisely these early Christian disciples, who found that their refusal to conform was deemed to be deeply offensive. This exposed them to ridicule and shaming.

> But recall the former days, when, after you were en-
> lightened, you endured a hard struggle with sufferings,

publicly exposed to reproach and affliction, and sometimes being partners with those so treated. For you had
compassion on those in prison, and you joyfully accepted
the plundering of your property, since you knew that you
yourselves had a better possession and an abiding one.[7]

Here the writer acknowledges that this Christian community has
suffered the ignominy of public shaming or reproach because of
their refusal to conform to the cultural expectations of them. To
experience shame was a devastating experience for it exposed the
sufferer to public disgrace and a huge loss of status.[8] In a society
that constructed itself around the two poles of honor and shame,
to lose face was to lose everything. The writer addresses this acute
pastoral situation by asserting that when Christ endured the cross
he faced the shame that was heaped upon him and counted it as
nothing:

And let us run with perseverance the race marked out
for us, fixing our eyes on Jesus, the pioneer and perfecter
of faith. For the joy set before him he endured the cross,
scorning its shame, and sat down at the right hand of the
throne of God.[9]

In *scorning shame* Christ inverted the normal cultural definition
of shame and in so doing asserted that true honor was to be found
elsewhere. It was not to be found in the approval of one's peers
through a conformity to cultural practice, but in the knowledge
that we are honored purely by being found to be in Christ and that
knowledge of our new found status is enough.

But how can it be enough? It is enough because being in Christ
means that our relationship with *time* is transformed. Culture, as
we have noted, is the expression of traditions and practices that
have emerged in history and are maintained as a means of social
cohesion. Cultures are transmitted from one generation such that
each generation takes on the mantle of being the guardian or the

7. Heb 10:30–39.

8 De Silva, "Honor and Shame," 521.

9. Heb 12:1–2.

curator of that culture. Cultural practice therefore ensures that the connection with those events and stories of the past is maintained. They re-enact the previous narratives in order to give meaning and value to the present. This works well provided that the members of society follow the rules and expectations and there is a degree of conformity. As soon as a segment of society begins to question the validity of cultural practices the possibility of social dislocation arises. This is precisely what occurred in the early centuries of the Christian history, which led to the waves of persecution under a number of Roman emperors.

When the gospel is understood to be radically subversive of all cultures, across time and geography, then a rigid adherence to the perpetuation of the past is called into question. It is my conviction therefore that the heart of the relationship between faith and culture turns around this issue of time. The early church struggled with this question. They were well aware of the notion of the regular, rhythmic, chronological passage of time *(chronos)*. They were aware too of those significant moments in time *(kairos)* when something of the presence of God breaks into our world. These *kairos* occasions occurred when the right time was reached. It may have been a moment of insight, an experience of conversion, or a dramatic intervention of the Holy Spirit. What they also needed to learn was that in Christ they now inhabited an entirely new dimension of time. This kind of time is referred to in the original Greek language as *aiōnios*. *Aiōnios* is usually translated into English as "eternity," which unfortunately carries with it the connotation of something which is everlasting or endless in duration. It is encapsulated in the ever-popular hymn "Amazing Grace," in which the final verse states:

> When we've been there ten thousand years,
> Bright shining as the sun,
> We've no less days to sing God's praise
> Than when we'd first begun.

A more accurate rendering of the sense of this Greek word is one in which time is understood more in terms of a *quality* of time than a duration. *Aiōnios* depicts the kind of time that God inhabits;

a beautiful timelessness, filled with the essence of the kingdom of heaven. Christian transformation, identity, and honor is discovered by means of dwelling simultaneously in two time dimensions. On the one hand, we have no choice but to dwell within our *chronos*, within the culture into which we were born and raised. This is our own incarnated presence in the world and we will unavoidably bear all the hallmarks and language of our cultural upbringing. Yet we also inhabit the *aiōnios* of God. We share in the kingdom of heaven and derive our true value and significance from dwelling in that utterly other dimension of time. It is because of this that we are empowered to hold on to our own culture lightly, not asking of it more than it can give us. We can celebrate many aspects of culture without demanding that it provide us what only God in Christ offers. It is the capacity to dwell in the eternity of God whilst remaining embedded in the *chronos* of the here and now that caused one New Testament writer to describe our experience as being *aliens* from another land who are resident here on earth.[10] This dual habitation is vitally necessary for our authentic Christian expression, yet it is a delicate and sensitive art to navigate between these two time zones. It is also profoundly subversive. It is what I would prefer to call "incarnational subversion."

If we look at one key issue with which the early church had to wrestle—the question of slavery—this subtle interplay between dwelling within a given culture yet simultaneously subverting it can be seen. Nowadays slavery is seen as self-evidently morally abhorrent. It is impossible for us in the twenty-first century to contemplate any ethical justification for the enslavement of one human being by another, and it is even more astonishing to note that it was tolerated and celebrated by vast swathes of the Christian church for centuries. It was not until the abolitionist movements of the eighteenth and early nineteenth centuries that Christians began to rethink their interpretation of the Scriptures. It is also perhaps surprising that the New Testament does not appear to overtly challenge the institution of slavery. If in Christ there is

10. 1 Pet 2:11.

"neither slave nor free"[11] one might have expected a more direct moral challenge to the institutional slavery of the Roman Empire into which the Christian church was born. Why the apparent reticence, one might ask, concerning this unambiguously unethical practice? If the gospel is intrinsically subversive then surely this is an obvious place to start?

As is so often the case things are not as simple and straightforward as they might appear to us at first. The culture of Mediterranean society at the time of Christ was deeply imbued with the presence of slaves. So deeply entrenched was the practice that it was inconceivable that economies could function without the vital role that slaves played. Indeed, some slaves were so well treated by their masters that they preferred to remain in the security of servitude even after their manumission had been granted. For some it was better to remain in the place where there was a roof over their head and food on the table than risk the uncertainty of the poverty of freedom. Slaves could have been asked to perform any task, ranging from the administrative duties of a civil servant requiring significant responsibilities to menial laboring jobs. It was in this cultural milieu that the fledgling Christian church found itself and questions soon arose concerning the status of slaves. The apostle Paul addresses the question of how faith in Christ and slavery as a cultural institution engage with each other at a number of different levels. Firstly, he does so out of pastoral concern for those members of the Christian church who were slaves. Secondly, he addresses the practice of slave trading, and thirdly, he speaks directly to the owners of slaves. We will look at each of these in turn. In his first letter to the Corinthians he addresses the pastoral needs of slaves themselves.

> Were you a slave when you were called? Don't let it trouble you—although, if you can gain your freedom, do so. For the one who was a slave when called to faith in the Lord is the Lord's freed person; similarly, the one who was free when called is Christ's slave. You were bought at a price; do not become slaves of human beings. Brothers and

11. Gal 2:28.

> sisters, each person, as responsible to God, should remain
> in the situation they were in when God called them.[12]

The key issue that Paul is addressing here is whether slaves should actively seek to change their status, from slave to free or—surprisingly—from free to slave. Paul was clearly unhappy with the practice of voluntarily selling oneself or one's family into slavery for the sake of paying off debts and he strongly discourages this practice here. If, on the other hand, the opportunity arose to gain freedom through being manumitted then he suggests that the chance should be seized. The central question, however, for Paul concerned one's identity in Christ. He states if you are in Christ you are already free, even though you may be a slave; and if you are free then you are, paradoxically, already a slave of Christ. Either way, it is your eternal *(aiōnios)* status in Christ that is more profound and more significant than your human status within society. As a Christian you already inhabit a different country—the kingdom of God—in which the normal understanding of time and the usual assessments of human dignity do not apply.

One may argue that this is not a particularly subversive position to take for it merely served to make slaves compliant and content with their lot. It was no doubt this kind of argument that persuaded Karl Marx centuries later to rail against the Christian faith as the opium of the people. Yet this advice from Paul was offered in a specific pastoral context in order to empower slaves in their position in society and to give them an inner dignity and honor that the prevailing culture could never have offered. His concern was not to make them compliant but to insist that their new found identity of being free in Christ was the foundation stone of their intrinsic honor. The longing for honor was, and remains today in most cultures across the globe, an essential component of the human condition. Once slaves truly experienced their honorable status in Christ then any desire to change one's status became of secondary concern. We must look elsewhere, therefore, for Paul's more subversive comments about slavery.

12. 1 Cor 7:21–24.

In his first letter to Timothy Paul needs to deal with a troubled
church in which the continuing role of the law was the touchstone
of controversy. There were those who insisted on the enduring pri-
macy of the law within the Christian church as well as those from
a Gentile background for whom the law held no such resonance.
So Paul writes to them and says;

> Now we know that the law is good, if one uses it legiti-
> mately. This means understanding that the law is laid
> down not for the innocent but for the lawless and dis-
> obedient, for the godless and sinful, for the unholy and
> profane, for those who kill their father or mother, for
> murderers, fornicators, sodomites, *slave-traders*, liars,
> perjurers, and whatever else is contrary to the sound
> teaching that conforms to the glorious gospel of the
> blessed God, which he entrusted to me.[13]

Here Paul lists slave traders along with murderers, fornicators,
liars, and perjurers. It is a formidable list and one which sent out
a clear signal, namely that if you were a member of the Christian
church it was simply not possible to participate in the economic
practice of buying and selling slaves. To do so would be to demean
and diminish the dignity of another human being for whom Christ
gave himself. By including slave traders in the list of vices Paul un-
dercut the whole economy of the slave trade, for without the con-
tinual buying and selling of slaves the practice could not continue.

The most telling piece of Paul's writing concerning the question of slavery, however, is contained in the beautiful pastoral letter to Philemon. Philemon was a leader in the church in Colossae,
a friend of Paul, and the owner of a slave called Onesimus. It is
clear from the way in which the letter is written that Onesimus had
stolen something from his owner, Philemon, and then immediately run away. He must have met Paul on his travels, experienced
a conversion, and subsequently became a fellow worker in Paul's
evangelistic endeavors. Paul and Onesimus had become close, so
close that Paul felt a deep filial love for him. It was the kind of
love that one might expect between a father and son. Now it was

13. 1 Tim 1:8–11.

time to send him back to his owner, hence the pastoral letter. Paul chooses to send Onesimus back, but with the urgent plea that Philemon should view this returned slave in a radically new way. Paul asked Philemon to do what humanly speaking was unthinkable, to embrace Onesimus as one would a long lost son. Indeed, he asked Philemon to give him the same honor as if it was Paul himself making a visit to Colossae.

Encapsulated in this very brief note is the compressed theology of Paul. He sees no distinction in status between himself, the educated former Jewish leader and teacher, and a runaway slave. Onesimus is not only now on an equal footing with Paul but he has also won Paul's heart. "I am sending him—who is my very heart—back to you," he writes. Paul has a thoroughly authentic passion for this runaway slave and it is his desire that Philemon receives him back into his household in the same manner. He does not simply want Philemon to forgive Onesimus for his misdemeanor, nor does he desire him to be merely tolerated, but rather welcomed into the household as a full member and as a son. Paul says that if Philemon is able to do this the he in effect welcomes Paul too, as if Paul is present in the person of Onesimus.

In making this plea Paul emphasizes that the good news of being found in Christ is that such wildly differing people as a slave owner and a slave now share fellowship *(koinōnia)* by virtue of the fact that they both equally belong to Christ. If they are both in Christ, just as Paul is also "in Onesimus," then a true and heartfelt welcome is not only possible, but necessary. One can only surmise how Philemon must have felt upon receiving this letter, which made such an urgent appeal. It would surely have turned his world upside down. The cultural expectation would have been that at the very least Onesimus would receive a beating if not lose his life for the crimes of theft and absconding. Yet now he was invited to enter an alternative kingdom where runaway slaves are treated as sons of the household. Paul's seemingly innocuous and tenderly written letter to one slave owner was, in reality, a highly subversive document, challenging the very foundations of society at the time.

Our guide at the outset of this chapter has been H. Richard Niebuhr, whose fivefold classification of types of Christian cultural engagement has formed the backdrop to this exploration. His categories are not meant to be rigid mental boxes, but merely stepping stones for contemplating this tangled issue. Plotting our own path in expressing our faith within the culture that we inhabit is a demanding task. It asks of us that we are able to stand back and view our own culture dispassionately from afar observing how its practices are rooted in history and how its values may be subtly shifting with each new generation. Our identity as *Resident Aliens,* to use a term coined by Stanley Hauerwas,[14] may prove to be the key that empowers us to view our own culture with a benevolent mistrust, knowing that the kingdom of heaven, our true home, is continually, quietly, and covertly breaking into our world.

14. Hauerwas, *Resident Aliens: Life in the Christian Colony.*

6

Other

Transformation does not usually happen in isolation, in the privacy of one's own life. It happens most powerfully in the company of others. These others may be an individual who functions for us like a beacon, someone who inspires us to reach beyond our limited horizons or someone who communicates that he or she believes in us. It is such people who offer us both the permission and encouragement to tread the path of transformation. Sometimes the significant other may present to us an alternative narrative of our lives, calling us forth to inhabit an entirely new story. Such people might begin sentences with such phrases as "I wonder what might happen if . . ." and they dream of alternative possibilities that inspire and elevate our souls. Others may even be those who are the source of intense irritation or disappointment for us thereby rendering our own transformation an urgent necessity. And sometimes our others are plural, a community to which we belong, however tentatively. The community itself becomes our significant other in which we are held, nurtured, protected, and urged on along the path of transformation. In my own life I can name a few significant individuals who have profoundly changed the direction that my life has taken.

Our guide in this chapter will be the German Jewish theologian Martin Buber, whose seminal work, *Ich und Du*, was published in 1923 and translated into English in 1937 as *I and Thou*. Buber was engaged with the quest to define what it meant to be fully human and in this, the most well known of his works, he makes the startling claim that *I-Thou* is a single word. It is not two words joined together by a hyphen, but a single entity, a noun, and Buber calls this a primary word. "The 'I' of man," says Buber is twofold, "in the beginning is relation—as category of being, readiness, grasping from, mould for the soul; it is the a priori of relation, the inborn Thou."[1] It is an assertion that our essence as human beings is only found in relationship with another. There is no such thing, claims Buber as the solitary "*I*." As soon as we insist on the validity and absolute necessity of our own private individual sense of identity we automatically reduce everything and everyone else around us to an object. What Buber was attempting to articulate was the complex relationship between subject and object, between me, the subject, and you, the object of my gaze. This subject-object conundrum has puzzled theologians and philosophers for centuries.

To the ordinary man and woman in the street this may seem about as interesting and as relevant as the attempt to calculate how many angels can sit on the end of a pin or whether the tree outside my window actually exists or not. The real world that most of us inhabit is dominated by the daily necessity of caring for our families and paying the bills, not with the abstract world of *I-Thou*. Yet it is worth pausing to consider these questions, for in reality they are not abstract at all.

When Buber claimed that whenever we insist on the priority and significance of *I* over and against *Thou* something dangerously tragic takes place. The *Thou* that faces us becomes an *It*. It is depersonalized and is thereby reduced to an object. When a person is reduced in this way then the outcomes are often violent and deadly. Witness, for example, the way in which victims of genocide are seen as less than fully human, as rats, as an infection, as units which can be—and often must be—destroyed. This is precisely what happened during the Third Reich in Germany in the 1930s when Jews, Gypsies, those with mental illnesses and homosexuals became *It*. As soon as such categories of people become an *It*, it is a very short step towards legitimized violence. Tragically this

1. Buber, *I and Thou*, 27.

story has been repeated time and again in history; in Rwanda, in Kosovo, in Afghanistan, in Syria. The only way that violence can be justified and explained is when the shift from *I-Thou* to *I-It* has been taken.

On a more individual level, the same dynamic is acted out whenever there is violence towards those who are different to us, who may be of a different race, a different faith, or a different gender. Sexual exploitation of women, for example, begins once the depersonalizing, objectifying process has already happened and women then become the tools, or the means, by which fantasies are played out or sexual needs satisfied. The shift from *I-Thou* to *I-It* is terrifyingly violent. Buber's assertion that "in the beginning is relation" is therefore highly pertinent, both to our sense of our own self and to the way in which we allow ourselves to participate in community. Buber writes that the DNA of our identity as humankind is illustrated by the way in which we come into the world. "The ante-natal life of the child is one purely natural combination, bodily interaction and flowing from one to the other."[2] The unborn child has no separate existence apart from its intimate connection with the mother. The two individuals are in fact one, the perfect depiction of *I-Thou*. We never need to move away from this unity of subject and object says Buber. We dare not do so, for if we do, we not only depersonalize the other but we also reduce ourselves to an isolated singleness, a person who has effectively ceased to be a person at all.

What Buber attempts to do is to sketch two landscapes, two habitats, in which one can dwell. One habitat is the world of *It*, the place of the known, the visible, and the place of objects that could perhaps be useful to us. The world of *It* is an environment of functionality and usefulness. It is often agenda-driven, with a defined goal or intention. In the world of *It* what matters most is defined by the final product, the profitability or usefulness of the encounter. *It* is all about purpose, achievement, and target. The world of *Thou* is wholly different to this. It is essentially a place of deep connection where vulnerable persons relate to other persons in the knowledge

2. Ibid., 25.

that our very being is only fully found in relation with the other who stands before me. It depicts a position where people face each other without agenda or ulterior motive. There is no functionality or utilitarianism in the world of I-*Thou*.

> No purpose intervenes between I and You, no greed and no anticipation; and longing itself is changed as it plunges from the dream into appearance. Every means is an obstacle. Only where all means have disintegrated encounters occur.[3]

Buber's assertion that true encounters between I and thou only occur when "all means have disappeared" is the kind of statement that sends a jolt through the reader. Many of the conversations and meetings between people are precisely that—full of "means" and objectives, where each person interacts with the other from a place of expectations, hoped-for outcomes, and prior judgments. Whenever this happens the encounter metamorphoses from a subject-to-subject encounter into a subject-to-object meeting. The "other" who faces us becomes objectified into someone, or indeed something, who might be useful to us. To eliminate any sign of "means" and to meet the other as a true "*Thou*" is to make oneself open to being transformed. The absence of "means" provides the door through which authenticity and vulnerability may make themselves known. Through that door another world beckons and it is in this place of connectedness we hear a call to become fully human, to become our true selves. Hear the words of Buber again as he sketches these two very different worlds.

> The world of *It* is set in the context of space and time.
> . . . [T]hese are the two basic privileges of the world of *It*.
> They move man to look on the world of *It* as the world in which he has to live, and in which it is comfortable to live, as the world indeed which offers him all manner of incitements and excitements, activity and knowledge. In this chronicle of solid benefits the moments of the *Thou* appear as strange, lyric, and dramatic episodes, seductive and magical, but tearing us away to dangerous extremes,

3. Ibid., 62–63.

loosening the well tried context, leaving more questions
than satisfaction behind them, shattering security.[4]

We do not need to look far in the pages of Scripture to illustrate this, for Buber's assertions have clear biblical resonances.
Even at the very moment of creation, God declares that it is not
good for Adam to live alone and that he needs a companion who
is fit for him. It is as if God is announcing that there is an incom-
pleteness about sheer individuality, that we only find out who we
are in the company of and before the face of another. The account
of the creation of humanity in Genesis 2 speaks of the way in
which Adam and Eve complement each other by providing deep
companionship. "For this reason a man will leave his father and
mother and be united to his wife, and they will become one flesh."[5]
The phrase that describes this unification has traditionally been
understood to have a sexual connotation. While there is undoubtedly a sexual implication here, the Hebrew word translated as
"united" (or in some versions, "clinging" or "cleaving") is the word
dābaq. In common usage it denotes strong kinship connection.[6]
James Brownson comments on this verse.

> The language of one-flesh is not simply a euphemistic
> way of speaking about sexual intercourse, it is a way of
> speaking about the kinship ties that are related to the
> union of man and woman in marriage, a union that in-
> cludes sexual intercourse.[7]

The oneness of this relationship echoes Buber's insistence
that humanity is constituted as a unity of the *I-Thou*. The notion
that there is such a being as a unitary and solitary *I* is absurd and
leads to a diminution of both *I* and *Thou*. The prophet Isaiah

---

4. Ibid., 33–34.

5. Gen 2:24.

6. Cf. 2 Sam 20:2. "So all the men of Israel deserted David to follow Sheba
son of Bikri. But the men of Judah stayed (*dābaq*) by their king all the way
from the Jordan to Jerusalem."

7. Brownson, *Bible Gender Sexuality*, 87.

announced this same truth about the oneness of the divine–human relationship.

> But Zion said, "The LORD has forsaken me, the LORD has forgotten me." Can a mother forget the baby at her breast and have no compassion on the child she has borne? Though she may forget, I will not forget you! See, I have engraved you on the palms of my hands; your walls are ever before me.[8]

The sense of desolation that the people felt in exile is uttered in the agonized cry that the "LORD has forsaken us, we are utterly alone, left to our own devices in a strange and foreign land." Isaiah steps into this situation to announce an alternative reality, one that is hidden from sight, but is nevertheless profoundly true testimony to the kind of relationship that already exists between God and his people. "We are joined together with God as a mother is with her new born child" asserts the prophet. "The connection is that intimate, that unbreakable. God has even taken an engraving tool and inscribed your name into his palms. You are written into the very fabric of God's existence and nothing can ever change or alter that." Isaiah is simply stating that from God's perspective the I-Thou relationship that he has with his people is indissoluble. He stands before us as the wholly Other, the original Thou, whose face is never ever turned away. It is only through a recognition of this, together with an experience of the depth of this intimate connection, that Zion can exist. That is the prophetic insistence that still makes its call to us today.

The intriguing story of the first encounter between Nathanael and Jesus is likewise revealing. It is recorded for us in John's Gospel, where we are given a description of a man steeped in the prejudicial stereotypes of his day. Upon hearing of the arrival of a stranger in his own locality the knee-jerk response from Nathanael is dismissive.

> The next day Jesus decided to leave for Galilee. Finding Philip, he said to him, "Follow me." Philip, like Andrew

8. Isa 49:14–15.

and Peter, was from the town of Bethsaida. Philip found Nathanael and told him, "We have found the one Moses wrote about in the Law, and about whom the prophets also wrote—Jesus of Nazareth, the son of Joseph." "Nazareth! Can anything good come from there?" Nathanael asked."Come and see," said Philip.[9]

When, however, Nathanael is taken to meet the stranger he is utterly disconcerted.

When Jesus saw Nathanael approaching, he said of him, "Here truly is an Israelite in whom there is no deceit." "How do you know me?" Nathanael asked. Jesus answered, "I saw you while you were still under the fig tree before Philip called you."[10]

If we use the language of Martin Buber to read this story, Nathanael strolls towards Jesus displaying the somewhat arrogant manner of a man familiar with an *I-It* perspective on the world. Within this worldview Jesus can be quickly categorized, for he comes from Nazareth, and everyone knows that such a town does not produce anyone worth listening to. Having been placed in this convenient category Jesus can be quickly diminished, and once this has happened he can then be discarded. Yet Jesus will not be so easily erased. Before Nathanael has time to utter a word Jesus calls out to him and in so doing looks through and beyond Nathanael's incipient racism. "Here is a man," declares Jesus "in whom there is no deceit." Jesus speaks the word *Thou* to him and evokes the response from within Nathanael that he is now, suddenly, fully known. "How do you know me?" he cries. Nathanael is being called forth into the fullness of life and that fullness begins and ends with being addressed as *Thou*.

What Jesus does here is an exercise in reflective interpretation. The person that Nathaniel presents is deeply unattractive. As he speaks he merely utters the epithets of the surrounding culture, rendering him less than the person he truly is. Jesus reflects back

9. John 1:46.
10. John 1:48.

to him, not a mirror image of those ugly attitudes, but the deeper truth that lies within Nathaniel, namely that he is a man in whom there is no guile and no deceit. It is a startling description of one who had, only seconds earlier, given such an impoverished account of himself.

The way in which the *I-Thou* dynamic functions lies precisely here in this interpretative role. In the space that exists between *I* and *Thou*, a world of interpretative possibilities exists. The *Thou* that stands before me can offer an entirely new perspective on *I*, reflecting back something *I* may not have seen in myself. *Thou* may say things and see things that remain invisible from the perspective of *I* but are dazzlingly clear from the vantage point of *Thou*. This is truly a divine gift. Yet, inevitably, the *Thou* that faces me may also at times present as someone abrasive, threatening, even alien to my well being. How can this *Thou* be part of God's gracious gifting?

The reality of the world in which we live is that our lives are filled with ordinariness. It is rare to meet an iconic figure who has the capacity to call us forth into the fullness of life. And if truth be told, it is all too common to encounter those who irritate, annoy, disappoint, and frustrate us. Buber's insistence that all human engagement be characterized by a beautiful, life-affirming *I-Thou* interaction is a challenge that needs to be negotiated if transformation is to have any lasting validity. His claim is that the other who stands beside me is a necessary and vital part of who I am, not a mere inconvenience to be brushed aside. I only know myself fully because I am intrinsically, unavoidably, essentially bound to *Thou* and *Thou* may not always be particularly beautiful.

Paul's letter to the Philippians, written from a prison cell, is surprisingly full of expressions of gratitude and may illustrate how he negotiated this path. In the first chapter of his letter he writes:

> Now I want you to know, brothers and sisters, that what has happened to me has actually served to advance the gospel. As a result, it has become clear throughout the whole palace guard and to everyone else that I am in chains for Christ. And because of my chains, most of the

brothers and sisters have become confident in the Lord and dare all the more to proclaim the gospel without fear. It is true that some preach Christ out of envy and rivalry, but others out of goodwill. The latter do so out of love, knowing that I am put here for the defense of the gospel. The former preach Christ out of selfish ambition, not sincerely, supposing that they can stir up trouble for me while I am in chains. But what does it matter? The important thing is that in every way, whether from false motives or true, Christ is preached. And because of this I rejoice.[11]

In his confinement Paul needs to deal with two sources of irritation. The first is that he languishes in prison with his freedom removed, surrounded by hostile guards, facing a highly uncertain future. Secondly, he hears news that alternative preachers have emerged who speak competitively with the intention of maligning the character and mission of Paul. He is surrounded therefore by what appear to be hostile "others." Yet these very sources of disruption to his life are the foundation for his gratitude. They are incorporated into the fabric of who Paul is rather than being wished away or dismissed. His imprisonment is the backdrop against which the truth about Paul, namely that his life is hidden in Christ, can now be seen with far greater clarity. His identity as a disciple of Christ is no longer obscured or in doubt, for the truth about Paul's identity is now evident, just as it became evident in the case of Nathaniel discussed earlier.

One of those interviewed for this project, David, narrated his story in which the role of significant others played a vital part. David was brought up by his grandmother after his mother had died at an early age. His father was not closely involved with the family. During his childhood and adolescence David suffered a number of abusive situations and times of neglect. The main source of solace during this period of his life was derived from the support and fellowship of his local Catholic church. By the time he was ready to leave school and go up to university he had experienced

11. Phil 1:12.

so much trauma at the hands of close relatives that he felt that the only option remaining for him was to deepen his trust in God. At university he was befriended by two other students from the Christian Union who showered him with compassion and acceptance. The liveliness of their personal faith was deeply attractive to David and contrasted with the more formal, liturgical Christianity that he had hitherto known. David describes this encounter in terms of "embodiment." They incarnated the reality of Christ and in so doing called him forth. He was able to see with his own eyes what redeemed, transformed human beings looked like, and it was profoundly attractive. Years later David entered a theological college where a similar encounter took place. One of the professors there perceived the potential that lay within David and, through persistent affirmation and encouragement, became for him a highly significant "other." During David's periods of self doubt and anxiety this professor consistently communicated to him that he was a person of intrinsic worth and dignity.

David's story illustrates how "others" impacted him in two opposite but complimentary ways. The abusive "others" of his childhood left David in a wounded and vulnerable state. His desperate search for a deeper divine reality in his life was the product of this period of trauma. The affirming "others" in later life were able to see the grace of God in David's life and embodied the voice of Christ through the way in which they encountered him. It is as if both types of "other" were necessary in David's journey towards transformation. David discovered the truth about who he was as a consequence of these encounters. Martin Buber writes tellingly about this emergence of I.

> Through the *Thou* a man becomes *I*. That which confronts him comes and disappears, relational events condense, then are scattered, and in the change consciousness of the unchanging partner, of the *I*, grows clear, and each time stronger.[12]

---

12. Buber, *I and Thou*, 28.

The gift of God to each of us comes in the shape of *Thou*, who may appear in many different shapes and sizes. Sometimes *Thou* presents in the form of a person who embodies the presence of Christ and at other times in the guise of an adversary. Both offer the opportunity to transform us into an authentic fully human *I*.

7

Silence

Silence is the gateway to the soul and the soul is the gateway to God.[1]

THIS FINAL CHAPTER OF our exploration into the dynamics of transformation deals with our relationship with silence. This may sound like a particularly quirky and abstract way in which to conclude this study. Previous chapters dealt with more tangible subjects—parental attachments, stories, pain, and culture—but silence? What can possibly be said about that? Silence, the absence of noise, the cessation of speech, how can this be an integral part of the process of transformation? Our guides through the silent land will be men and women of the fourth and fifth centuries who devoted much of their lives to silent, contemplative prayer. These desert fathers and mothers believed that a great deal could be said about silence. So who were they?

In the early fourth century the minority, persecuted, underground Christian church experienced a reversal in its fortunes. In the year 313 AD Emperor Constantine declared Christianity to be the official religion of the Roman Empire, thereby transforming its status from a dangerous, subversive sect to a respectable part of the establishment. Persecution of the Christian church vanished, but in the wake of this new era of approval the church faced entirely new challenges. Now the Christian communities needed to find

1. Fr. Christopher Jamison, BBC TV series *The Big Silence* (2010).

out what it meant to remain distinctively Christian at the centre of civic life. How could they maintain their prophetic edge in a climate of state endorsed approval? The danger of easy compromise with the powers-that-be was all too evident to one young man living in the small Egyptian village of Coma. One day, in the year 269 AD, he heard the gospel read aloud which announced "sell all you have give to the poor and you will have treasures in heaven." That young man was Anthony of Egypt and upon hearing the scripture he felt a call to obey this injunction wholeheartedly. He left his home village and made his way into the Egyptian wilderness simply to listen to the voice of God.

Anthony spent the remainder of his long life in the desert, dying in the year 356 at the age of 105. The model of his monastic existence inspired thousands to follow his example and within 100 years of his death monastic communities had sprung up throughout the Egyptian and Syrian deserts, reaching even to France, under the guidance of the hermit John Cassian. The wisdom that these austere men and women acquired through their silent desert lives has been collected in various *Sayings of the Desert Fathers and Mothers* and it is from these epithets of wisdom that we will draw as we explore the world of silence.

Silence has a curious, pervasive existence. We all know that silence is there, ever present, although it is mostly kept firmly in the background of our lives. Whether we like it or not, all of us have to negotiate our own relationship with silence. One way of forming this relationship is to fill the spaces with noise. Digital technology, for all of its wonderful benefits, is particularly well suited to blocking out the hovering, brooding presence of silence. If we don't want to hear the silence it is easy enough with a flick of a switch or the touch of a screen to eliminate it. Or one can simply keep busy. A life filled with one appointment after another, meals taken on the go, the urgent necessity to cram into each twenty-four-hour period as much as possible is a sure fire way to leave no spaces, no gaps, nowhere for silence to make an entrance. Michael, one of those interviewed for this project, comments honestly on his ambivalent relationship with silence.

I generally avoid it as much as possible. I'm the eternal extrovert who is always looking for a conversation, a dance, some fun. But, I am also drawn to silence. I have been on a number of silent retreats. I'm terrible at them! I end up sleeping for the first thirty-six hours, or take long walks and sing or try to sneak off with someone or read books. And yet it is in silence that I can write and hear God while writing. I can pray for a while. In my retirement, my phone almost never rings and I don't have many people showing up on my doorstep. I spend a lot of time alone. Surprisingly I don't listen to much music and I spend more time with silence than I used to. I watch more stupid TV than I should. I also want to explore the silence of God question.

Silence waits for us. It is not easily dispensed with, for it is always simply there and sooner or later we will have to decide what to do with it. The trouble with silence is that is not really silent at all. Those who have ever attempted to sit with eyes closed in complete silence even for ten minutes will know what a noisy place it is. Very soon a horde of seemingly random thoughts and feelings arrive with alarming force. They contain stories of events of long ago or of an incident that might have only taken place during breakfast this morning. There may be fantasies, imagined future scenarios, conversations we might have had or we could perhaps have had. And with each of these thoughts it is surprisingly easy to add a commentary, a note of self-recrimination or regret or a few paragraphs perhaps of self-justification and revenge. Silence can be a noisy, scary place, which is why many of us do our utmost to avoid it for much of our lives.

The desert fathers and mothers were utterly convinced that there could be no genuine, deep transformation into the likeness of Christ without time spent in silent prayer. The sayings of the desert fathers have come down to us in the form of short aphorisms and stories about incidents and conversations that took place between a desert abbot and another brother or spiritual seeker. Here is a typical example.

A certain brother went to Abbot Moses in Scete, and
asked him for a good word. And the elder said to him: Go,
sit in your cell, and your cell will teach you everything.[2]

The cell might have been a small hut or cave in which the hermit
spent much of his time. It was precisely there in the cell, utterly
alone, that he was faced with the demons and fantasies that arrived
unbidden within his consciousness. Despite his simple intention
to be in the presence of God, Abbot Moses found that his sacred
cell was frequently invaded by wild, unwanted distractions. In
that space he was confronted with himself, with the raw, ragged,
internal muddle that accompanied him even into the far reaches
of the desert. This cell became, therefore, the place of encounter
with himself and through that struggle, with God. That is why Abbot Moses was able to reply to the enquiring brother, "your cell
will teach you everything." If you stay there with the noisy cocktail
party inside your mind and don't run away seeking distractions,
then you will learn the essence of transformation.

But why should that be the case? What could possibly be the
benefit of coming face-to-face with our own demons, that mad
swirl of our own minds? The answer lies in learning to find our
deepest identity in God yet knowing that that discovery is hin-
dered by layers upon layers of false selves. The way of silent prayer
begins with the recognition that our lives are already hidden in
Christ and Christ is already in us. We are held in the embrace of
the Father, Son, and Holy Spirit. It is the exact opposite of a striv-
ing upwards towards a holy and distant God. Rather, it is in the
realization that God is not "out there" somewhere, but deep within
us already. That is our true home. That is the place of belonging.
That is where we find ourselves. The process of arriving at that
deep place of knowing the love of Christ is a progressive shedding
or letting go of our over-identification with the random, haphaz-
ard thoughts and feelings that knock so loudly on the door of our
cell. It is absurdly easy to believe that those fleeting thoughts and
ridiculous commentaries are depictions of who we truly are. The

2. Ward, *Sayings of the Desert Fathers*, 118.

desert fathers knew that that was a lie. Such thoughts come and go like clouds skidding across the horizon. They are ephemeral apparitions that present themselves as alarmingly real and utterly true.

The discrepancy between the solidity of our true identity and the transitory nature of our false selves is captured by the poet in Psalm 125. "Those who trust in The Lord are like Mount Zion which cannot be moved." It is this solidity that our true identity in God offers. Our identity is as sure and solid as a mountain and the noisy thoughts that accompany us during times of silent prayer are merely passing clouds around Mount Zion. They appear for a moment or two and in a few short minutes they are gone again. To identify with this "weather" and to confidently declare "that is me" is a foolish deception and it was something of which the desert fathers and mothers were acutely aware. Martin Laird in his book *Into the Silent Land,* writes perceptively about the Psalmist's metaphor.

> We are the mountain. Weather is happening—delightful sunshine, dull sky or destructive storm—this is undeniable. But if we think we are the weather happening on Mount Zion . . . then the fundamental truth of our union with God remains obscured and our sense of painful alienation heightened.[3]

The kind of silence that the desert monastics sought was beautiful, healing, and creative. It is the silence that God entered on the seventh day of creation and the silence that speaks of the rest to which the writer of the book of Hebrews urges us to enter.[4] It is a silence that opens out onto new vistas, the silence of the presence of God's grace, the kind of silence that sharpens the senses and enables connections with others.

Over the centuries of Christian history of silent prayer, two related but slightly different emphases have emerged. One is

3. Laird, *Into the Silent Land,* 16.

4. Heb 4:9–11. "There remains, then, a Sabbath-rest for the people of God; for anyone who enters God's rest also rests from their works, just as God did from his. Let us, therefore, make every effort to enter that rest, so that no one will perish by following their example of disobedience."

sometimes known as apophatic prayer or the prayer of negation. It is a kind of prayer that is highly intentional in that the person praying seeks to orientate her or his soul towards the presence of God and in so doing seeks to simply "be" there. It is wordless prayer, a prayer of facing towards, often accompanied by a prayer word or prayer phrase. The ancient "Jesus prayer" still used in many Orthodox churches is a good example of this. This kind of prayer does not seek to focus on anything other than being present before God, without agenda, demand, or petition. It gently lets go of all the passing mental debris that floats past and attempts to return to the anchorage that is the Trinitarian embrace. The negation that characterizes this approach to silence is not an austere, ascetic, denial of anything and everything that is pleasurable. Rather, it is the releasing of all that interrupts, clouds, or distorts an intimate union with God. It does not rigorously attempt to control the mind, but in repeated actions of intentional gentleness always returns to a place of silent, wordless rest.

An alternative to apophatic prayer is kataphatic prayer. This kind of prayer is usually associated with Ignatian spirituality. Ignatian spirituality invites us to imaginatively enter the world of the text, to make ourselves present in the biblical stories and to notice our own affective responses to what unfolds. It is a prayerful reading of the words of Scripture so that we inhabit them and become participants in the unfolding drama of the text. This approach is more active than the prayer of "letting go," yet it also depends on purposeful periods of silence. Both apophatic and kataphatic prayer are entry points into the silent land where our own tongues are at last stilled. One of the desert fathers, Abba Tithoes, stated that "to be on a pilgrimage is to be silent and those on a pilgrimage should control their tongue."[5] The desert fathers were all too aware that it is our speech that so often gets us into trouble, speech that does not emanate from a silent heart, but from the turmoil and agitation that lies within all of us. The silence of the desert, whilst being a place of the most intense struggle, was

5. Ward, *The Sayings of the Desert Fathers*, 198.

essentially a beautiful silence which was capable of producing beautiful transformation.

There is, however, another kind of silence that is not healthy. It is the silence of those who simply cannot speak, for their pain is too great. My observation of this kind of silence has emerged from my experience of living and working in southern Germany as the minister of a church. In this role I had contact with many who had stories to tell about the impact of the Second World War on contemporary German society. I have heard tales of young men who returned to German society at the end of the war, having been conscripted and forced to fight for the Nazis. They had been compelled at gunpoint to commit unspeakable acts of violence against their fellow human beings. Some of them had been posted to the Russian front and witnessed unimaginable scenes of human devastation. Upon their return many were simply too traumatized and humiliated to speak of their experiences. Some just sat in a corner of their homes silently for years. Almost all were utterly unable to communicate what they had endured to those nearest to them. Their silence sat heavily upon their families as a brooding dark presence, needing to be broken open to allow healing and restoration to be given a chance. I know of several adult Germans, currently in their fifties, who regularly experience prolonged periods of chronic depression and *ennui*. They sense that such times of darkness can be traced back to their early childhood experiences of being in the presence of their shamed, silent relatives.

There is yet another form of silence that is known mostly by women. It is the silence that often seems to accompany sexual violence against them, and such silence is usually intensely and ferociously private. Those women who have suffered the violent invasion of rape often testify to the desperate need to preserve a veil of silence over the whole sordid business. Theirs is a silence of humiliation, a grey blanket that covers over a tragic episode in their lives. Or it is the silence of terror resulting from the overt—or sometimes insinuated threats—of the perpetrators. To live in such a silent world is not a place of comfort, although it may appear at least to be a place of imagined safety. Some rape victims even leave their own homeland and emigrate to another land where another language is spoken. In that new land they can distance themselves from the place of violation, they learn to speak again, but it is not their mother tongue. They construct an entirely new identity for themselves. The person who was raped remains back there from whence they came and is silent. Nancy Venable Raine, herself a victim of sexual violence, articulates the shocking nature of her toxic silence in her book *After Silence: Rape and my Journey back*:

> Silence has the rusty taste of shame. The words "shut up" are the most terrible words I know. I cannot hear them without feeling cold to the bone. The man who raped me spat these words out over and over during the hours of my attack. . . . It seemed to me that for seven years—until at last I spoke—these words had sunk into my soul and become prophecy. And it seems to me now that these words, the brutish message of tyrants, preserve the darkness that still covers this pervasive crime. The real shame, as I have learned, is to consent to them.[6]

This is the landscape of toxic silence. Such silence may be rooted in the shame of deeds committed against another or conversely in the shame of being a victim. It can enter a soul by a mere word or phrase, it can have a shocking longevity, it can thoroughly tarnish and spoil the fullness of life that Christ came to offer. Silence that is associated with shame is of an entirely different order. It is a fearful, closed silence—imposed either from without or from within, it matters not—a silence that dare not be broken for fear of further humiliation. It is the silence that makes you want to run away and hide, that builds impregnable walls between you and others who might dare to venture too close. Those who know the power of shame know intuitively about this kind of violent silence that shouts at us that we are not worth hearing and that our voices must be drowned out. The silent shamed live in a world of their own, feeling, thinking, choosing like everyone else, but not daring to articulate. It is life inside a cage where no one really knows what is going on.

6. Raine, *After Silence*, 6.

For the contemporary reader the story of king Nebuchadnez-zar in Daniel 4 is one of the more bizarre biblical narratives. It tells of an articulate and powerful ruler who has a disturbing dream. It is only Daniel, the exiled Israelite, who is able to interpret the dream for him and informs him of the nature of God's impending dealings with him. In due course, Nebuchadnezzar suffers exactly what the dream had foretold and finds himself driven away from society, living as a wild animal. The modern reader may dismiss this tale as absurd and of no contemporary relevance. Yet the in-sights of the French philosopher Paul Ricoeur, whom we met in an earlier chapter, may be apposite at this juncture. Ricoeur in-sisted that readers must beware of standing over a text and decid-ing beforehand what is in the realm of the possible and what is not. Such an approach limits the power of texts to communicate. Remaining within the world of the text itself by contrast, allows the text to have its own voice and thereby to make utterance. It is to suspend the usual boundaries of the real and the fictional, the normal and the supra-normal. Allowing the text its own authentic voice, emerging from its own unique context, gives space for "an overflow of possibilities."

If we heed this advice when approaching Daniel 4 we can perhaps hear the story with the ears of a contemporary listener. Nebuchadnezzar is portrayed as the ultimate symbol of human ar-rogance. He is an invincible ruler whose power no one could imag-ine ever being diminished. Yet, in the hands of the skillful Hebrew storyteller we read of his sudden and dramatic humbling. Some-how, by the miraculous power of God, Nebuchadnezzar is shamed before his own people and driven out into the wild. There he loses the power of speech and ends up in a bestial condition. What is the narrative intent of the storyteller at this point? Undoubtedly there is a theological motif running through this tale demonstrating to a group of shamed Jewish exiles in Babylon that the power of Yahweh is infinitely greater than any human empire. Yet the storyteller also pairs together the humiliation of Nebuchadnezzar with his own silencing out in the fields. Out there he has no voice, not simply because there is no one to listen to him, but more fundamentally because he can no longer speak. We are left to draw the conclusion that the story depicts the concurrence of shame and silence. Once Nebuchadnezzar is silenced out in the wild his power to dominate and terrify through his rhetoric is nullified.

A further story concerns the woman who reached out and touched the hem of Jesus' garment as he passed by.[7] Luke recounts the story and portrays her as suffering from bleeding for many years. We are not told the cause of this medical condition, but one can easily imagine the shame and humiliation it would have caused her. She would have been considered unclean and therefore set apart from full inclusion in society. As she approaches Jesus she does so in stark contrast to blind Bartimaus. His was a very noisy intervention: hers was entirely silent. She does not draw attention to herself and even when Jesus stops to enquire who had touched him she continues with her attempts to conceal her true identity. The story depicts her as being highly agitated, falling trembling at the feet of Jesus, unable to remain silent any longer. One can sense that she has lived in a silent world of shame for many years and that she had hoped that she could be delivered from her curse in a silent manner. Yet this was not possible. Jesus demands that her plight be seen and her desperate, silent cry for help be heard. Not only was she healed of her physical condition through this encounter but her silence was broken and her position of dignity within the community restored.

If shame can produce such terrifying silence, in what way did the ministry of Jesus address this? The writers of the Synoptic Gospels all depict the ministry of Jesus as being framed by two significant periods of silence. The first occurs in the immediate aftermath of the baptism of Jesus as he is driven out into the desert by the Holy Spirit, alone, where he spends forty days in a silence broken only by conversations with the devil. It is this extended period of solitude that is the necessary precursor to his public ministry. This is a creative silence that is extremely demanding, yet ultimately profoundly fruitful. The questions posed by Satan were existential ones, turning around the one central issue concerning the identity

7. Luke 8:40–48.

of Jesus. "Who do you think you are?" the satanic voice screams. It is a voice that is still heard by the those who suffer in toxic silence to this day. The question posed implies that our own identity is flawed or that we live a false and meaningless life, absolved of any right to existence. The old satanic question is profoundly contemporary. Jesus meets the question head on and rebuffs it, repeatedly refusing to accede to the temptation to capitulate. His period of desert silence was to be the platform for the subsequent empowering of his ministry.

The second period of silence for Jesus takes place during the last hours of his life and the rhetorical intent of the Synoptic writers is thus highly suggestive. The two periods of silence form bookends for his ministry. It is as if silence is the framework within which he makes his public utterances. Jesus stands before Pilate at his trial with accusations being hurled at him. In response Jesus remains silent, making no attempt to defend or explain himself. Throughout the previous three years he had taught in the synagogues, he had spoken out courageously before the powers that be, he had told parables to impoverished peasants. Yet this moment was the moment of silence. All of his ministry had been spent seeking out and noticing the shamed, the marginalized, and the excluded. He stood with them, walked beside them, and understood them. And now, at the denouement of his time on earth, he chose to enter their shame-filled silence too.

How can we offer an interpretation of this silence? His silence on this occasion appears to be of a totally different order to the silence of the desert during his time of temptation. This was not the silent listening for the voice of the Father, nor was it a silence which encountered demonic whisperings in his ear. It was however the dignified silence of someone who was fully in control of his own choices in the face of sadistic and unjust treatment. In one sense, he was a passive victim of the judicial process, but simultaneously he was an active participant in his own destiny. The story of his trial is a tale of the struggle for power, which, as we have already seen, is often the key issue that lies at the heart of shame-based silence. The Roman authorities were convinced of the validity and impregnability of their own power base. The inhabitants of the land of Israel, which had been occupied, likewise perceived the Roman occupation as one that was supremely self-assured and therefore unassailable. Pilate attempts to convince Jesus that all the power of the Roman Empire lies ranged against him. It is the language of the bully and the oppressor, yet Jesus steadfastly refuses to accept this perception of the balance of power and in so doing despises the shame that is being heaped upon him. The question of who possesses power becomes one of the central issues in the trial of Christ. No less is true for many today. Power is often given away to those who are perceived to be greater than us, even if that perception is utterly at variance with reality. Power is a relative not an absolute commodity.

In theological terms the silence of Jesus was the continuation of the trajectory of his entire ministry, which was driven by the passionate desire to seek and to save the lost. He had always sat beside those who were shamed and excluded and those whose voices had been extinguished. His behavior at this trial was a further manifestation of this orientation. It was his identification with their silent world. During those fearful moments of trial and crucifixion he chose to absorb within his own body their silent terror. Yet his chosen silence also proved to be the fulfillment of an ancient prophecy.

> He was oppressed and afflicted, yet he did not open his mouth; he was led like a lamb to the slaughter, and as a sheep before its shearers is silent, so he did not open his mouth.[8]

The silence of Christ at his trial is mirrored by the silence of God the Father during the most acute moments of Christ's passion. As he falls to his knees in the garden of Gethsemane, pleading for the cup of suffering to be taken from him, what sound is heard from heaven? Nothing. As he hangs on the cross and senses that the face of his Father is turned away, he cries out "my God, my God why have you forsaken me?" What is the answer from heaven

---

8. Isa 53:7.

to that piercing question? Silence. Barbara Brown Taylor writes tellingly about the silence of God at the moment of crucifixion.

> From the cross he pleaded for a word, any word, from the God he could no longer hear. He asked for bread and got a stone. . . . Will anyone suggest that God was simply not listening? I do not think so. In the silence following his death, Jesus became the best possible companion for those whose prayers are not answered, who would give anything just to hear God call them by name. . . . The God who keeps silence even when God's own flesh and blood is begging for a word is a God beyond anyone's control.[9]

There is one intriguing reference to God's silence in the book of Revelation. The apocalyptic vision includes the opening of seven seals by the Lamb. The culmination of this process takes place when the seventh and final seal is opened, at which point the writer, John, states that "there was silence in heaven for about half an hour."[10] The opening of the final seal appears to signify the conclusion of the work of God in Christ, which is symbolized by a period of silence. We are not given many clues as to how to interpret this final silence. The most convincing interpretation in my view has been put forward by Israel Knohl,[11] who asserts that the silence in heaven referred to in Revelation 8 has echoes of temple worship in which the burning of incense was usually done in silence. This view is supported by the story of Zechariah in Luke 1:9–10. Zechariah takes his turn to go into the holy of holies to burn incense, while the assembled worshippers remained *outside* praying. Inside the temple, with Zechariah, one can imagine the awe-filled silence that was present. The apocalyptic silence in Revelation 8 has the sense of a holy, healing, redemptive silence, a silence that draws into itself all other silences, however toxic they may be. The Bible begins in silence. Before the voice of God called creation into being, there was simply the Spirit of God hovering silently over the

9. Taylor, *When God Is Silent*, 512–14.

10. Rev 8:1.

11. Knohl, "There was Silence in Heaven," 512.

waters. At the conclusion of biblical narratives we return to that silence where all things are renewed and restored.

This chapter began with an introduction to our guides in the land of silence, the desert fathers and mothers of fourth-century Egypt. Having fled from the noise and bustle of the city and found a home in the vastness of the desert, they discovered that intentional silence before God was a way of waiting, watching, listening, and noticing all that lies within as well as all that surrounds us. By way of analogy, it is the spaces that lie between the notes in a piece of music that are just as fundamental as the notes that are played. Without those spaces music would simply be noise. The desert monastics yearned to explore those silent spaces knowing that God is often silent and it is precisely in that place that he can be found. Macarius the Great, one of the desert fathers, was born in 300 AD and was greatly influenced by Anthony of Egypt. He spent much of his time in the desert travelling from place to place, eventually settling in a desert hermitage at Scetis. It may be fitting therefore in concluding this chapter to allow Macarius to have the final word. On one occasion he spoke to his fellow monks saying:

> Flee my brothers. One of the old men asked him, "where could we flee to beyond this desert?" He put his finger on his lips and said, "Flee that" and he went into his cell, shut the door and sat down.[12]

---

12. Ward, *The Sayings of the Desert Fathers*, 110. Macarius saying, No. 16.

The Transforming Gaze

ON A RECENT VISIT to Chester Cathedral I was struck by the powerful "Water of Life" sculpture in the cloisters of the cathedral grounds. The sculpture depicts the encounter between Jesus and the Samaritan woman at the well recorded for us in John 4. The artist, Stephen Broadbent, has chosen to place the woman above Christ offering him fresh water and Christ in turn both receives this gift and offers her the water of life. Both are giving and receiving from each other, and between them lies the gaze, a gaze that I imagine would have elicited that woman's transformation.

This exploration into the hidden dynamics of transformation has traversed a range of landscapes. We have explored the tricky process of honoring our parents while also being prepared to allow ourselves to compassionately detach ourselves from them. We have examined the way in which language and stories have shaped who we are and who we might become. Our journey has taken us through the place of discomfort and we have attempted to sketch the contours of silence, all the while trying to negotiate our path through the tangle of tradition and culture. But perhaps the most significant piece of this mosaic is that we are bound to the other, to someone who is not us yet is an essential part of who we are. We are constituted as people-in-relation and it is those relations with the other that exert the power to both transform and to destroy. It is the presence of the face of the other that is so existentially necessary. As Buber has asserted, "all real living is meeting."[1] The Water of Life Sculpture depicts this and encapsulates many of the themes this book has attempted to explore. It does so with devastating simplicity. It is the simplicity of the gaze.

At first glance it is a surprising, unnerving sculpture. The position of the woman is unexpected, for she is placed above Christ, looking down at him. Christ is found beneath her in a receptive pose, or at least in such a way that the woman is not placed in a typically subservient role. Their two bodies are connected together at the feet making one sweeping, beautiful, united arc. The artist has thereby created a venue for an encounter to take place. Admittedly, this is all the product of one artist's imagination, for we have no way of knowing how the conversation actually took place. But what the artist invites us to do is to enter the scene with our own imagination fully engaged, the sculpture being the stage upon which our minds and hearts may perform their work.

I wonder what the gaze might convey. Maybe for her it is the gaze of love, of being seen and accepted as she is with her checkered history with men, with her exclusion from the community where she lives, with her nationality as a despised Samaritan. All of this is known to Christ as he looks at her with eyes of compassion.

1. Buber, *I and Thou*, 25.

And what does her gaze convey to him? Do you really know me? How can you treat me with such dignity and honor? Are you—a man—willing to accept what I am offering? The mutual gaze is mysteriously beautiful and we know from the Gospel account that after this encounter the woman rushes back to her community with an energy and a joy that was baffling to those who knew her. Maybe it was the language of "water of life" that engaged her soul or perhaps it was the beginning of a new narrative of hope replacing the previous story of shame. Could it be that her painful history had prepared an open and receptive heart within her? Maybe it was all of these things.

What the sculpture communicates is that the transforming gaze is not, in the first instance, a rational, logical or even a linguistic event. We began this study by pondering the phrase "Be transformed by the renewal of your mind," noting as we did so that "mind" does not equate to rationality. Paul's use of the Greek word *nous* does not carry with it any of the associated Greek philosophical presuppositions of logical deduction. Paul was steeped in the Hebrew mindset in which mind, body, and soul were always viewed as a whole, a single entity, in which one part was intimately infused with all other parts. The gaze of Christ towards the Samaritan woman at the well was an act of knowing, of recognition, and of affirmation. The gaze and the verbal exchange that accompanied it entered the soul of the woman at a deep place of emotional and spiritual need. It was from that place of renewal and cleansing that she was able to truly hear the announcement of newness from Christ. That announcement declared that the place of encounter with God was not to be found in that which was deemed to be geographically sacred. Rather the declaration contained the astonishing words that it was within her own soul, that place which hitherto had been abused, shamed and sullied, that true worship was to emanate. And it was precisely from here that the unending, living, spring of the water of life would flow.

Whilst it is possible to say that the encounter was not in the first instance a rational one, this does not discount the rightful place of rationality, persuasion, and learning. All of these took place for the woman at the well, although they were the outcome, rather than the precondition, of the gaze. This book has attempted to sketch the contours of that process of digesting and making sense of any kind of transformative encounter with God. It may not—and most times does not—begin with a simple rational exercise in deductive reasoning. Transformation takes place because we have been approached and touched by God at his initiative. Our response to this divine dance is to deploy all our faculties; emotional, narrative, psychological, rational, volitional, and spiritual to ensure that such transformational opportunities become rooted and grounded in the love of God and are allowed to bear their beautiful fruits in due time.

Reflections

Permission

How could you depict the quality of your attachment to your early care givers?

Are there any similar patterns of attachment in the way you form relationships today?

How does your experience of the Fatherhood of God speak to your attachment patterns?

Discomfort

What is your typical response to discomfort or pain?

Has your experience of discomfort deepened your faith or reframed it or diminished it?

Narrative

Consider how you tell the story of your life.

How does the story change when different people are listening?

Can you tell your story in such a way that you include the embrace of God: Father, Son, and Holy Spirit?

Language

Are there biblical metaphors that speak to you strongly?

Are there biblical metaphors that leave you untouched?

Can you explain the difference?

Culture

Are there aspects of your own culture that you find delightful?

Are there aspects of your culture that you find distressing or disturbing?

What does being "incarnationally subversive" mean in your context?

Other

Who have been the "significant others" for you?

How have "significant others" called you forth into the fullness of life?

Imagine how you could be a "significant other" for someone else. What would that look like?

Silence

What relationship do you have with silence?

Is silence a place of presence or absence for you?

Do you sense a call towards greater silence?

Bibliography

Augustine, Saint. *Confessions,* New York: Barnes and Noble, 2007.

Bonhoeffer, Dietrich. *Letters and Papers from Prison.* London: Fontana, 1953.

Bowlby, John. *Attachment and Loss. Vol 1.* London: Penguin, 1969.

Brownson, James. *Bible Gender Sexuality: Reframing the Church's Debate on Same Sex Relationships.* Grand Rapid: Eerdmans, 2013.

Brueggeman, Walter. *The Message of the Psalms.* Minneapolis: Augsburg, 1984.

Buber, Martin. *I and Thou.* Edinburgh: T. & T. Clark, 1942.

deSilva, David A. "Honor and Shame." In *Dictionary of New Testament Background,* edited by Craig Evans and Stanley Porter, 518–22. Downers Grove, IL: IVP Academic, 1997.

Hauerwas, Stanley. *Resident Aliens: Life in the Christian Colony.* Nashville: Abingdon, 2014.

Ignatius of Loyola. *Spiritual Exercises and Selected Works.* New York: Paulist, 1991.

Kappes, Marcianne. *Track of the Mystic: The Spirituality of Jessica Powers.* Lanham, MD: Rowman & Littlefield, 1994.

Knohl, Israel. "'There was Silence in Heaven' (Revelation 8.1): An Annotation to Israel Knohl's 'Between Voice and Silence.'" *Journal of Biblical Literature* 117.3 (1998) 512–14.

Labor, Tim. *Wittgenstein and Theology.* London: T. & T. Clarke, 2009.

Laird, Martin. *Into the Silent Land.* London: DLT, 2006.

Lewis, C. S. *The Problem of Pain,* London: Centenary, 1940.

MacMurray, John. *Freedom in the Modern World.* London: Faber & Faber, 1945.

Niebuhr, Richard. *Christ and Culture.* New York: Harper and Row, 1951.

Powers, Jessica. *The Selected Poetry of Jessica Powers.* Washington, DC: ICS, 1989.

Rahner, Karl, and Paul Imhof. *Ignatius of Loyola.* London: Collins, 1978.

Raine, Nancy Venable. *After Silence: Rape and my Journey back*: New York: Broadway, 1999.

Ramshaw, Gail. *Liturgical Language: Keeping it Metaphoric, Making it Inclusive.* American Essays in Liturgy Series. Collegeville, MN: Liturgical, 1996.

Ricoeur, Paul. *Figuring the Sacred.* Minneapolis: Fortress, 1995.

———. *Oneself as Another.* Chicago: University of Chicago Press, 1992.

———. *Time and Narrative, Volume 1.* Chicago: University of Chicago Press, 1990.

Semujanga, Josias. "Religious Discourse and the Making of Dualistic Identity." In *Origins of the Rwandan Genocide*, 71. New York: Humanity, 2003.

Taylor, Barbara Brown. *When God Is Silent.* Norwich: Canterbury, 2013.

Vanhoozer, Kevin. *Biblical Narrative in the Philosophy of Paul Ricoeur.* Cambridge: Cambridge University Press, 1990.

Ward, Benedicta. *The Sayings of the Desert Fathers.* London: Mowbrays, 1975.

Wittgenstein, Ludwig. *Philosophical Investigations.* Online: http://gormendizer. co.za/wp-content/uploads/2010/06/Ludwig.Wittgenstein.Philosophical. Investigations.pdf.

———. *Remarks on the Foundations of Mathematics.* Edited and translated by G. H. von Wright, Rush Rhees, and G. E. M. Anscombe. Oxford: Blackwell, 1978.